Leadership vs. Management
How to motivate and develop our team's capabilities through effective communication, coaching, and training

Zack McQueen

Text Copyright © Zack McQueen

All rights are reserved.

No segment of this book can be used again in any form without the publisher's written consent except in the case of brief quotes in critiques or reviews.

Legal Disclaimer

The info in this book and its contents is not designed to replace or take any form of health or expert advice. It is not meant to replace the need for private medical, financial, legal, or other professional advice or services, as may be needed. The content and info in this book have been offered for the learning and entertainment of the reader.

The content and info in this book have been compiled from sources deemed reliable. It is correct to the best of the author's knowledge, research, and belief. On the other hand, the author cannot guarantee its accuracy and validity and cannot be held liable for any errors and lapses. Furthermore, changes are periodically made to this book as and when needed.

When you use the contents and information in this book, you agree to hold harmless the author from and against any harms and costs. And this includes any legal fees potentially resulting from applying any of the info offered by this book. This rider applies to any loss, damages, or injury caused by the use and application, whether directly or indirectly. It also applies to any advice or info cited, whether for personal injury, tort, breach of contract, negligence, criminal intent, or under any other cause of action.

You agree to accept all risks of using the information presented inside this book.

You also agree that by continuing to read this book, if appropriate and necessary, you shall consult a professional. This professional can be your doctor, attorney, financial advisor, or any such other advisor as needed. And this is best done before using any of the suggested remedies, techniques, or information in this book.

Table of Contents

Introduction

Chapter 1: What Makes a Leader Different from a Manager?

    Focus

    Skillset

    Vision

Chapter 2: Common Grounds

    Communication

    Decision-making and Problem-solving

    Crisis and Change Management

    Time Management

    Emotional Intelligence

Chapter 3: Shared Skills

    Communication

    Delegation

    Motivation

Chapter 4: What Makes a Good Manager?

    Commercial awareness

    Forward planning

    Interpersonal skills

    Mentoring

    Organization

    Problem-solving

    Strategic thinking

Chapter 5: Qualities of a Leaders

    Commitment

    Creativity

    Feedback

    Flexibility

    Positivity

    Responsibility

    Trustworthiness

Chapter 6: Unleashing the Leader in You

Chapter 7: Inspirational Leadership

Chapter 8: Your Personal Journey

Chapter 9: Setting Free your Team's Full Potential

    Communication

    Coaching

    Training

Conclusion

Introduction

When I was doing my MBA, I got fascinated with the topics of leadership and management. If you are checking out this book, then I believe you, too, find them a fascinating subject. So, here I am, sharing with you my different perspective on the topic. I will be using a combination of examples and practical advice as to what you need to do to become a successful leader who people believe in and like to follow.

We all know that many of today's companies are looking for leaders, be it in the role of store supervisors or senior managers in large companies. There is this constant search for leaders out there, but very little is known about how one can be a leader. Are you curious about where do leaders get their experience from? In reality, I think, most of the time, you are just asked to "manage" your colleagues, not really "leading" them.

As a result, you never really get to be the leader the company and colleagues want. I know of someone who has managed many people and departments for years but told me that she does not consider herself a leader. When asked why she feels that way, her response was mind-blowing:

"I don't think I really inspire them to follow me. Yes, my staff follow me to do assigned tasks, knowing I will check their work. That makes me a manager, not a leader."

Here is a practical guide on how you can become a leader, someone who motivates people to do their best. I pray this book can make you go beyond being an excellent old manager who makes sure a task list is completed and everyone's started work on time.

Rest assured that you will see the increased productivity, retention, and engagement of your people in your journey to becoming a leader, besides nurturing future leaders. And everything starts with your decision to get a copy of this book to guide you in your journey...

Chapter 1: What Makes a Leader Different from a Manager?

We often cannot distinguish a leader from a manager as these terms are used interchangeably. Although there are some areas at work where their work overlap, there, too, are significant differences. For one, the definition of leadership and management are not the same. Leadership is defined as making positive change that includes the formation of an idea to lead that change.

This idea is actually a strategy to empower people to create the vision into a reality despite the obstacles. And this entails the foundation of a merging of resources and drive that can push that change onward. In contrast, management is defined as getting the baffled, misguided, lazy, and misdirected people to carry out a common goal on a steady, recurring basis.

So, in an organization, the leader may, for example, gives direction or guidance for the company to be able to sell stocks to the public. With this goal in mind, the managers will plan for getting this done. Take note, though, that some people may lead devoid of a managerial position, while some managers do not lead at all. Hence, a manager can be found atop the organizational chart while leaders are all over the same chart.

This denotes that managers may not be a leader. Still, the leader is a manager with or without such a designated position backing him up. Perhaps, this is because a manager generally exists as someone who's selected, if not appointed, in an organization. Typically, a manager is chosen based on his specific knowledge, technical skills, and expertise. And upon joining a company, the manager automatically has people who really do not have much choice but follow him.

In contrast, leaders just shine through amidst the crowd. They grow "fans" or a cluster of people who admire and follow them willingly. In organizations, having both great managers and leaders is essential.

Good leaders are needed to direct the organization towards achieving its purpose and vision. And to compliment these leaders, good managers are essential to make sure that things stay done and teams are in line with the organization's set goals. To further differentiate a leader from a manager, let us consider these three aspects.

Focus

As just pointed out, leaders unite resources while managers align efforts with the company mission and vision. This entails the leader to innovate, develop, and focus on the workforce. Leaders do not focus so much on the way of organizing people to do the needed work. Instead, they focus more on discovering ways to support and inspire them.

This makes the leader's central function as mobilizing others to execute a series of distinct and collective undertakings. By adopting a unique leadership style that emphasizes honest feedback and self-reflection, leaders can find better ways to inspire their employees to believe in.

And this is on top of them pursuing vital company initiatives! So, it is evident that leaders focus on ideas or on looking for chances for progress on the company level. They do this by presenting new ideas, as well as driving the change to an avant-garde mindset. These ideas are primarily the result of leaders looking for answers to questions starting with "what" and their respective reasons.

In terms of interacting with people in the organization, the leaders communicate in a more high-level yet empathetic way. And this is because the focus of a leader's attention is on what must be done towards achieving more significant results. As leaders look for innovative ideas, they also possess a crucial part in driving shifts within organizations.

What is more, a leader triggers positive, slow changes by empowering workers to work for common goals. And the most potent means of leaders for doing this is efficient interaction. After all, change communication comes from leaders. And to get the people prepared to carry out things differently, the leader has to give the rationale behind the change.

This places leaders in a great position of power to enthuse people. And once again, by adopting a particular leadership style that stresses continuous feedback, self-reflection, and authentic interaction, leaders can energize their workforce. And not only that! It can also enable them to catch their fans' attention and motivate them to follow necessary organizational plans. Also, workers feel less pressured at work when they can regularly interact with leaders. Thus, a leader also has an impact on employee engagement. I remember a friend of mine told me that her work calendar included having lunch with the company CEO once a month.

I was amazed! Considering that her CEO is a foreign national who is the CEO of a Tokyo company, he must be doing a great job juggling his daily work schedule. Also, free lunch is always a welcome treat to all employees, right? So, I asked my friend how she felt having lunch with her boss monthly.

She said that her monthly lunch date with her boss allowed her to clarify some company issues. It also gave her the chance to explain some cultural gaps that generally happen in a multinational company. In terms of the free food that can cause a smile on the workers' faces, she told me that their office pantry really gives free lunch to all employees during working days.

When specific teams are required to go overtime for days, they give three free square meals each day. That privilege is only given to full-time employees, though. Still, I know that her company has more than 50 full-time, so isn't that startling? She told me that a separate team takes charge of that but admits that preparing food for more than 50 people Monday to Friday is a feat.

As a worker, you get to focus on finishing the job without skipping your meals and even looking for food to eat. Wow! I already want to work there! My reaction made her laugh. She added that it was really the two-way communication and input sharing that inspired her to work well.

I told her how lucky she is for having a boss who supports open, honest, and plain communication. Of course, that is on top of their work culture that clearly shows how much they value their workers! Indeed, the leader has shaped well their company culture that the managers endorse.

We all know that each company has a specific culture representing its system of standards, beliefs, and conduct. This culture shapes and determines how a company operates and the manner of getting work done. When the organizational culture stays aligned towards the overall company strategy, employees, besides other stakeholders, behave and act in a supportive way to reach business targets.

It stands as the leader's job to sustain the firm culture's core business values and mindset in their actions, genuine interaction, and choices. Inspiring and ardent leaders greatly influence sharing the firm's culture throughout its people that influence their actions. Their skills and style of leading indeed impact how the workers take and abide by that culture.

Then again, driving staff towards living by their culture and central values can only happen with leaders' and managers' group effort. Sadly, many companies today neglect the importance of two-way communication amid workers or managers and leaders. Hence, we often see the information flowing down to the employees without the chance for them to join the company's conversation or knowing the reason for changes in the organization.

Meanwhile, the manager directs, maintains, and centers his efforts on the process and structure of carrying out tasks. Managers pursue the goals of a firm through synchronized actions. Planned routes, events, and tasks unfold over phases to get hold of a precise result.

The most common example is when managers carry out an approach to decide something when heading a vital exchange of ideas or relay a change within the firm. Also, it should be noted that the firm's culture highlights control and reason. So, naturally, managers always search for solutions on timelines, ways, and means.

This makes the managers' prime burden as living up to their tasks founded on their leader's vision. Their main work is to safeguard that workers on different roles with different accountabilities work productively while feeling that they can realize the objective.

In the process, they always keep an eye on the outcome by controlling workers and providing needed information, techniques, and tools to properly succeed. Of course, managers interact with people depending on their function in the decision-making process. And this is simply because their focus is on how things are done.

In terms of company culture, managers direct their employees towards adjusting to it as shaped by the leader. So, it is the role of the manager to continuously endorse and support this culture within teams. It is sad to note, though, that while managers constantly reinforce the change communication messages, some managers do not really understand the reason for the change.

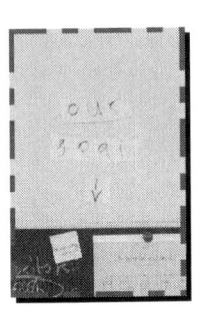

In worse scenarios, some managers may not even be aware of the change that is happening. Still, they hold the task of driving their people to continuous success and getting helpful work experience during their entire career. As managers are responsible for more than 70% of staff engagement at work, they, too, are held answerable for how well and sound their teams stay. The saddest part is when workers are not motivated by what leaders say, there is nothing much managers can carry out to facilitate their people's success.

Skillset

As we will discuss this topic in detail in another chapter, we'll just discuss this briefly. Foremost of all, managers and leaders possess some different characteristics and skills. And this is because they often have overlapping roles in an organization. Then again, both share common grounds, which we will also discuss in another chapter.

For leaders, though, their most excellent skill lies in their power to inspire and influence. To do this, they do not need a specific position in the company. So, we can see workers who are not managers but do quality work due to actions that inspire or engage other workers.

Perhaps, each one of us is born into the world with some level of leadership. This quality needs shaping, though, through growing emotional intelligence. Also, learning the subtle way of influencing others, each of us, irrespective of our professionalism level, can build better self-awareness that can help us understand the way to draw out the finest in ourselves and others. For both aspiring and seasoned managers, having solid leadership skills leads to better work performance. On top of that, they acquire improved learning of the proper way of winning over the environment wherein decisions are made.

Vision

An effective leader is aligned on the vision to drive change and more bent on thinking in advance and making the most of whatever opportunities come their way. With that said, we can safely deduce that leadership is on working out what the targets should be. So, it's more on driving change. And this change is set on a vision that managers follow.

Take note that, in terms of setting and carrying out a company's vision and mission, leaders and managers have different functions. Most leaders have a solid mental picture of wherever they wish their firms to be within the next five or 10 years. They understand, though, that they aren't the only people responsible for turning their vision into reality.

So, by speaking frankly about the company's goals, prospects, and challenges, leaders stay responsible for building faith in the office. They foster a helpful work environment for employees to feel inspired to impart their own thoughts, needs, and worries. And the more visible the leaders remain, the better the work setting becomes.

The future vision may mean nothing, though, when the leader cannot clearly explain it to the bosses and workers. Thus, every leader must strive towards making that sense of drive among workers. After all, among the massive "pushers" of staff stanchness and action within the workplace stands as purpose, besides matching workers' work and personal values.

In contrast, bosses embark on meeting the firm's goals by way of carrying out a course of action. For example, the Finance Manager takes care of budgeting, while the Administrative Manager handles the staffing and corporate structuring. Then the managers of each department work with one another to ensure that the company's objectives are executed.

As a whole, it's the practice of functioning with others towards ensuring the practical carrying out of a preferred array of goals. And this is where managers have a crucial part. In a nutshell, it can be summed up into this:

- Leaders are responsible for sharing the vision, mission, and plans to the whole company workers through helpful leadership interaction.
- Managers hold the burden of keeping employees in line with their central goals and values.

> Stuborn
> on
> Vision
>
> Flexible
> on
> Details.

Unfortunately, today's surveys reveal that 71% of workers think their respective leaders don't spend ample time communicating goals and programs. As a result, even when managers influence people towards working on the same goals, many employees concur that they fail to share their visions.

At the end of the day, workers expect and would very much appreciate it if they know how their company is doing and where it's heading. And as the leaders plan for the future, the managers tackle the present. So, in terms of vision, leaders look at tomorrow while managers look at today.

I'm sure that you now have a pretty good idea of how a leader is different from a manager. As I have mentioned, both hold functions that overlap at some points in an organization. We will now discuss the common grounds between the two.

Chapter 2: Common Grounds

We are now aware of the distinct roles and burdens of a leader and a manager. Still, there exists an innate gray area between the skills, duties, and traits that each needs. In the next chapter, we will tackle their shared skills. So, for now, we will discuss the gray areas of their responsibilities. I also will include specific topics, specifically time management and emotional intelligence, which I have observed stand imperative to both leaders and managers, although at varying levels.

Leaders and managers are equally necessary for any group's success within today's gradually more complex and erratic commercial environment. In fact, many organizations stay overly managed that causes them to stagnate. And the reason for this is because the company is governed by processes that exclude the human touch. In contrast, overly-led companies can create chaos and instability because it does not have systems in place.

Alas! This is a standard modern setting for many working people in the 21st century. For thriving business groups, though, it has been observed that they could make the distinction between leaders and managers quite clear. They keep both of them in their firm while finding chances to improve and guide these likely leaders simultaneously. Now, let us look at the three salient areas common to both leaders and managers.

Communication

The critical communication skill of leaders is their ability to pay attention when someone is talking to them. This includes listening to what is said and left unsaid. The unspoken words are usually represented by the feelings behind the spoken words. Of course, the leader also considers the related questions asked on the message conveyed. On the other hand, managers usually do one-way messages through the use of accepted communication forms, like press releases, bulletin announcements, memos, and a more formal customized letter.

Despite the contrast in how they connect with their people, communications from both the leaders and managers are vital for a business's success. As mentioned in the previous chapter, workers look forward to being informed and prepared for what their firm stands for and intends to achieve. While leaders interact to motivate people, the managers' constant and precise messages empower people to perform at their best, besides building stronger relations amid teams.

Decision-making and Problem-solving

Great leaders know how to even out feelings with reason and make choices that are helpful to themselves, their staff, clients, shareholders, and the business. Generally, we view leaders as those who can quickly decide and communicate them with the goal in mind to others.

Perhaps this is because influential leaders can quickly put two and two together and map out a realistic action plan ahead of time. They possess an approach that serves by way of a foundation for the way problems are tackled and managed. Also, they tend to anticipate things that may happen out of the blue and utilize their people's strengths to ensure the strategy causes a sustainable way out.

Managers, on the other hand, are constantly asked to make choices when solving problems. For them, making decisions and solving problems are ongoing activities. This covers evaluating circumstances, considering alternatives, deciding, and following up on the needed actions.

It follows, therefore, that the process of solving problems of managers is a constant cycle of setting up, doing, checking, besides acting, while likewise keeping an eye on the state of affairs and outcomes. As may be needed, managers tweak their plans to move forward for the target result that will direct them towards better business outcomes sooner or later.

We can clearly see that making good choices and solving problems are shared burdens of both managers and leaders. While leaders cover making decisions on a top-level, managers take charge of making decisions on the department level.

Crisis and Change Management

The top leaders take private ownership during a crisis, even when many factors and issues lie beyond their control. When a problem happens in the firm, they align team effort right away, set up unique metrics to check the output of workers, and build, if not strengthen, the culture of responsibility. During such a period, leaders stay watchful and in line with a daily dashboard on main concerns. Meanwhile, leaders offer the inspiration to change and get people involved when doing change management.

They produce the sense of need and importance of change, besides showing commitment and delight about things getting done. In reality, leaders know that change is difficult; and, thus, understand that people need the motivation to leave their respective comfort zones. In contrast, managers manage a crisis in the company by creating a plan, designating a spokesperson, and remaining transparent and frank about the issue.

They also inform their staff of all pertinent facts and keep the communication lines with suppliers and clients open. What's more, they ensure the release of early and frequent updates through social media and other excellent communication forms. When managing organizational change, managers clearly state the change needed and align it to company goals.

Also, they bear the burden of finding out the impacts and those influenced by the modification. They foster a communication approach, provide needed training, employ a support system, and measure the process of change. Thus, we can safely deduce that just like the other areas, managers and leaders work hand in hand when a change is needed, or a crisis occurs in the company.

The current situation in the world today taught us the value of agile work transformation, besides the demand to quickly adjust to change. Except for some industries, many workers have started to work from home to manage the impact of the COVID pandemic. While leaders might have an enhanced grasp of the adjustment that needs implementation, managers have excellent knowledge around the proper way to enable employees to agree to the change, besides aligning with it.

Of course, in general, the world is forced to work from home and stay at home knowing that their life is at stake. In this case, leaders support the work from home scheme to lead their people towards the common goal, which is protecting lives. In terms of managing workers from home and controlling the workflow, the managers have no choice but to face the challenges.

Whichever way, both the leaders and managers are assets to all organizations. Just as it's equally vital to know that there no one is born to take on a specific role, being a leader or a manager demands skills to be acquired, as well as honed. Ideally, each function is interdependent, but appreciating their differences and similarities is an excellent jump-start to further develop ourselves.

Time Management

In terms of time management skills, all leaders and managers are, for the most part, juggling their work hours amid three fundamental pursuits. These are:

1. Leading, which is the strategic features of their position.
2. Managing, which means working with other people to get the desired results.
3. Doing, which is the actual carrying out of tasks.

Irrespective of their role, both leaders and managers need to spend some time mull over and work out future organizational essentials. And this must take in the truths of today's impact on workers brought about by the health crisis, technological changes, and the business's complexity.

To face these challenges, managers and leaders must evaluate how they devote their time to matching these competing actions. It cannot be denied that finding how to spread your time exists as key to business success and your own career growth. Can you tell me at this point how you are managing your time?

When was the last time you have undertaken an honest evaluation of how you allocate your time covering the three areas cited in your current distinct role? Is there a need for you to stop doing some things or start doing something to balance your time among tasks and, perhaps, move you nearer your desired professional path?

Emotional Intelligence

In my honest opinion, the ultimate node between a leader and a manager is the appreciation of what motivates, as well as causing individuals to act in the manner they do. Of course, this includes their skill of dragging out the finest in each staff according to the intended purpose.

To do this, you must be emotionally intelligent. After all, organizations consist of people. And with people involved, emotions come into the picture without any doubt. So, this is a standard case in all workplaces. I have never seen a workplace devoid of any feeling in my years of working.

Also, I have not witnessed a company that is all objective and performance-focused. How about you? Have you experienced being in a room packed with people where hormones do not creep in even the slightest way?

I guess this is only possible when you are surrounded by robots, not people. Unlike robots, people's emotions, by themselves, are the main factor of motivation or de-motivation. I hate to admit it, but emotions alone direct the carrying out and quality of any worker's output.

If you do not believe me for saying this, then allow me to remind you of its link to the need and value of balancing work and life. And if you still do not agree with me, why do we need emotionally intelligent managers or leaders? The current eras are very full of life, not just in terms of business dealings but also in a social context.

Due to the fast intro of hi-tech gadgets into our lives, the social structure is rapidly going forward to the speeding up of trades and movements all over the planet. This includes goods, human resources, services, funding, tools, and social habits. And among its effects is its helping and boosting contact between diverse regions and peoples around the world.

Hence, the mean workforce age is going down with the leaders or managers now looking forward to having people from various backgrounds and cultures work with them. In this setting, it is crucial to be highly subtle when dealing with people's emotional facets. In essence, EI or emotional intelligence remains the power to make out and fathom one's own feelings and those of other people. And this insight must be used in a way to manage moods and relations.

As stated, you can simply deduce that EI covers four crucial aspects: awareness of one's self, managing one's self, social awareness, and social skills, or working on relations. Knowing that a leader or a manager has a massive impact on their people's drive and thoughts, being emotionally intelligent must be a shared trait.

Honing this trait will further the gift of a leader or manager to enthuse trust and optimism in their followers or workers. This will empower them to take on constructive endeavors, called resonance. In contrast, the lack of this trait in leaders or managers can negatively impact workers to destruction, such as what the world saw in Adolf Hitler's life.

Also, EI is vital since followers or workers count on it from leaders or managers. A staff reporting directly to the manager or leader would require him to know his state of affairs and priorities. Whether the manager or leader does or does not know these things, this affects his commitment level and work performance in his people's eyes.

Sometimes, it is awkward to tackle the emotional sides of dealings between people. Still, leaders and managers need to know the relevance and importance of emotions as it holds a vast effect on the work outcomes. While doing reviews and training, the comments have to be given acceptably.

The leader or manager must be conscious of his workers' worries and self-doubt that are sometimes expressed or kept hidden. The higher the position level a person has in a company, the more vital it is to clearly define his anxieties, which the leader or manager must anticipate.

Finally, to attract and keep talented and motivated workers, a leader or manager needs to go over his EI and people skills. The soonest we accept that no one comes into the world with the charm to manage or lead people, the easier it is for us to develop ourselves. Fortunately, EI with diligent practice and wisely directed hard work can be fostered.

Coming up next is our discussion on the shared skills of leaders and managers. I deliberately included EI in this chapter as a form of opener for what we will talk about next. This is because your EI level can impact how you go about your skills in communicating, delegating, and motivating your people. Let us continue…

Chapter 3: Shared Skills

As a manager or leader, you are expected to know your own strengths and weaknesses. This is because your staff may find it challenging to take in guidance from someone who is unmindful and not sentient. When a person portrays any of the two roles in an organization, he has to empathize with the circumstances, emotions, aspirations, besides reasons of his people.

For example, a decreasing output of a member of his team might be due to some reasons. It can be that a disruptive staff is facing motivation problems. Another reason may be that a subordinate known to use abusive words with others at the workplace might lack support in his personal abilities. In such cases, the leader or manager needs to detect the facts and attempt to reach deeper into your skills to understand things that are not obvious. Given this scenario, both managers and leaders need to possess the following skills to effectively function.

Communication

We have touched on this earlier, but allow me to dig deeper into the topic. People in leadership and management ranks must often practice suitable communication knacks with their people to be effective. Displaying strong communication skills fosters trust, instills drive, and helps workers reach their potentials in terms of work output.

Take note that people in positions are closely watched by rank and file employees regarding their facial expressions, body language, and many more. So, they need to study both their verbal and non-verbal expressions. They should discern if any of the two forms are causing harm or positively influencing other people in the workplace.

For instance, if you are talking about business ethics with a touch of doubt and a dazed look on your face, your audience can see that and may cause your message not to be received well. After all, a person with a station in a firm must always behave as a model. His movements, therefore, must aptly support his statements, beliefs, and standards at all times.

Through communication skills, people occupying specific posts in a company form clear influences among members of the company, fostering a robust sense of spirit. From interacting with workers to keeping other officers updated on daily actions, leaders and managers must effectively convey messages in various ways with every type of people. Indeed, communication skills stay essential for the following reasons:

1. Ensure communication routes among all employees remain effective and open;
2. Help employees stay focused on objectives and desired outcomes;
3. Increase the work output of personnel;
4. Make every staff aware of his responsibilities in the company; and,
5. Promote teamwork among members and amid teams.

Here are a few communication flairs that account for more good working outcomes:

Active listening

This skill remains a person's knack to focus solely on the speaker and comprehend what he is saying. Obviously, this denotes that you hold on to what he is telling you and understanding the message relayed. Through this ability, you can provide valuable answers and make sure that your staff feels heard and understood.

This happens when you paraphrase what was said, you ask open-ended or probing questions, or you voice out short affirmations. Another technique employed is recalling previously shared knowledge.

Adaptability

Learning this starts with the full knowledge that not all personnel speaks by the same token. Hence, people with work titles must know how to adapt towards meeting the various kinds of exchanging of ideas that their workers prefer. Being flexible makes it possible for you to adjust your interaction to ensure that you have a mutual understanding between you and your people.

Being open-minded will help you develop this trait, which is also an essential factor in practicing practical communication skills in the workplace. Open-mindedness lets you hear what other people are saying without even trying to tweak their thoughts or beliefs. This facilitates your complete understanding of what they are saying and helps you create educated decisions.

Empathy

Frankly, I view this as a virtue and not just a skill. Practicing this allows personnel to be very receptive to whatever you are saying. Also, empathy helps you absorb what the employees feel that responding to their requests becomes easy. When you practice openness and authenticity in speaking with your people, you are building trust at the end of the day.

To enhance staff retention, many managers and leaders have to be empathetic. Also, you cannot lead or manage people who you do not understand. And your power to influence and inspire people can only occur when you are aware of their feelings. With empathy in your dealing with people, you can fathom the core cause behind your staff's poor work output.

Empathy can also endow you with what is needed to help employees strive, improve, and do exceptionally well. As a result, you can build, besides develop, rapports with those you lead. And for this reason, empathy is crucial in the workplace. Aside from its being a thinking and emotional muscle that grows stronger with daily use, it is vital for managers and leaders alike in terms of competency.

Now, how can you practice empathy often? One way to develop empathy with your team is to create a personal link with your team members. For example, international organizations, such as UNESCO and World Bank, use effective interaction in their dealings through empathy towards understanding work culture to enhance staff effectiveness. Many current behavioral and educational studies promote effective exchange of ideas through compassion, enhancing work effectiveness and supporting resilience.

Nonverbal communication

Likewise, leaders must know the proper way to effectively express themselves nonverbally, such as through their facial expressions, body language, and actions. When you perfect the art of matching your unspoken and spoken communication style, you can easily make your listener understand what you wish to convey.

For instance, when you are standing up straight and making eye contact when speaking to someone, you give a positive message. Now, how about when you are managing or leading people online? We cannot deny that the worldwide COVID 19 disease made speaking in the cyber realm become a regular part of many leaders' and managers' daily work.

Our knowledge of managing or leading is acted out in these milieus, mainly in channels that involve only text, stays very partial. In the case of spontaneous occurring text conversations, the question is: What can leaders and managers use in place of nonverbal communication skills to do an array of complex interaction goals?

Can managers and leaders complete work while fostering ease and friendly concern, besides creating the feeling of an actual, not virtual, teamwork between members using instant or text messages? A study revealed that it can be done by learning the language and nonverbal means the virtual world offers in work settings.

So, by building knowledge of how nonverbal communication exists vital even in this realm, we can convey subtle cues. Take note, though, that virtual teamwork is only doing well if the manager or leader can:

1. Resolve miscommunication issues,
2. Adopt an interactional style that is positive, and

3. Make possible a helpful working environment.

Of course, with visual and audio tools, such as Google Meet or Zoom, managers and leaders today do their duties. With instant messages, face-to-face speechless interactions are re-formed through pictures, icons showing feelings, and glyph. Unlike wordless hints in speech, they are used freely at all times, reworked creatively, as well as relying on the speakers' know-how of previous chatting contexts in written or spoken dealings.

Standard samples include typing a word in capital letters to stress it or having a thumbs up or smile sign after the written words. The focused usage of voiceless signs to review social intent is to express in code feelings and ease, evoke effects using sounds or icons to show thoughts.

These cyber cues highlight, clarify, flick through the meaning, or convey the status of importance. Hence, virtual leaders and managers must use language, besides communicating skillfully, physically, and virtually.

Positivity

Positively sharing ideas can very much affect your people's drive, as a whole, and the way they receive info coming from you. Speaking and moving with optimism can establish a pattern for your people that will encourage them towards doing the same at work.

A stern test facing today's leaders and managers is getting their people's trust and seeing them helpful in tackling change amidst the turmoil. Indeed, we face taxing times that the level of clearness and bright outlook of leaders and managers impact their perceived trust, besides assessing their value. Although it is difficult to maintain positive verbal and wordless communication, always remember that employees closely watch you. So, even when you just received awful news and your people are around, do your best to act positively.

Never underestimate how swift news travel among workers. Then again, we all see how the economy is greatly affected by the pandemic. And to support social distancing, staying home, and wearing protective masks initiatives, countless businesses today had to layoff almost 50% of their workers.

So, how can managers or leaders announce a layoff positively? Under such circumstances, it is best to first find any outplacement program you can offer to the worker you are about to release. Then, have a private meeting with the staff involved. When talking to the person, keep your message to the point because employees can get the news right away.

Don't worry too much because it is common knowledge that a RIF or reduction in force is needed for many companies to survive the economic impact of COVID. Still, show your empathy by finding ways to support the affected worker in the transition.

Storytelling

This is among the latest communication tool that even social media platforms use in conveying their messages. Perhaps this is because it effectively builds trust, makes connections, and moves others to react to what is said. The storytelling types include giving value propositions and launching a mission, besides empowering other people in the workplace.

Telling stories aids in creating meaning that can be disclosed among colleagues in a much more superb way. Also, you can learn so much by taking note of your employees' stories as they can include any concern or issue they are wrestling with. The main benefits of using storytelling when communicating to your people are:

1. Can energize, persuade, and entertain the person you are talking with;
2. Cause moving memories that can stay for a long time;
3. Easier to recall than figures or data; and,
4. Help in establishing credibility and truth.

Through telling stories, leaders and managers can adapt them to handle today's most awkward challenges that can:

1. Create highly performing teams,

2. Convey you as a person,

3. Enhance your charm,

4. Get people enthusiastic on a needed major change,

5. Inspire people towards acting in exceptional manners,

6. Manage or lead people,

7. Share knowledge,

8. Spark change,

9. Translate abstract and dry numbers into gripping pictures of goals, and

10. Transmit values.

Delegation

This shared skill consists of working with staff to establish focus, command, and responsibility. As a matter of fact, the person delegating authority retains the blame, should anything go wrong, even when completing the task is assigned to subordinates. Its purpose is to give leaders and managers free time to direct their effort on higher-value pursuits.

So, when you delegate work, you can employ time more usefully, such as strategic planning. Also, it allows you to direct your attention to other duties that cannot be delegated, like coaching team members. Thus, as a leader or manager, you must suitably know when you need to do things personally and assign tasks. You must be aware of when team members stay acting as a single unit and when differences exist. A straightforward task delegation is an essential part of good leadership or management communication.

It calls for you to take time to explain why you picked a person or a team to do a particular work and your expectations of them. You have to understand that many people prefer knowing what they remain to do and its purpose. By giving your staff this information, you can further inspire them to become as prolific as possible.

If you are curious if you are delegating tasks effectively, you must first know your people's strengths, weak points, and preferences. This knowledge is essential when choosing the right team or person to do a task. This will help you explain why you are delegating.

Also, provide precise and correct instructions, resources, and, if needed, training. As you explain the task, answer the questions that start with "when," "who," "what," "why," "where," and "how." When talking about deadlines, explaining its reason because the workers may not know that their work is only a slice of a range of tasks representing a big job.

Make sure to assign duty with its matching clout. You must check the commissioned work regularly to discuss progress and give feedback. When the task is done or is continually done well, never forget to thank the person doing the job. In reality, effective delegation alters the perspective from working on tasks and following processes to training employees to do well in their work.

It engages staff as responsible allies in tasks, jobs, and objectives instead of simple pieces of human business resources. Delegating can also sometimes be complicated as it requires the principal skill of self-awareness and negotiation. This means that you must be aware of your preferred control level and your staff's work preferences.

Then, you must strive to pinpoint a balance amid the two towards letting your staff grow in his job. You can learn the control level people like by asking them and negotiating the delegation-level that you employ with them to arrive at a win-win setting.

Motivation

Good leaders and managers know the proper way of motivating their people through communication. It is crucial to discern what inspires your members and employ this knowledge within your interactions with them. In a nutshell, motivation remains a goal-oriented trait that helps persons achieve their aims.

It pushes them to knuckle down at achieving set goals. Hence, managers and leaders must possess the right traits to affect motivation. There is, however, no specific outline for inspiration other than keeping an open viewpoint on the nature of humans. Hence, knowing the different wants of your people can, without a doubt, make the process of making decisions easier.

A vital guideline that outlines motivation's fundamental belief is harmonizing and matching the subordinate wants with the company needs. This denotes that you make sure that the company shares the same mores and standards that you seek in your employees.

You must ensure that your people are heartened and coached in a way that meets business needs. Giving credit and gifts are prime driving forces that sway a person towards meeting the desired target. Rewarding good and exceptional behavior through a letter, certificate, or small gesture of appreciation is a significant influence.

If you opt to issue a certificate, always make sure it mentions the particular action or the excellence wherein the individual exists being rewarded. On the other hand, being a model for your people to follow is likewise a critical reason influencing them to reach their goals.

Also, you should set yourself as a decent standard to ensure your people will grow and attain their goals well. Cheering workers towards solving major issues can inspire and teach them the ins and outs of crucial aspects of making judgments. What is more, it helps all to know their role better in the business.

The exchange of ideas will be transparent and will indeed attract acknowledgment, besides pleasure from top management. Meanwhile, developing team spirit and morale certainly holds a pivotal effect on the business well-being. After all, the mental or emotional status of any person constitutes his moral fabric.

Since your actions and judgments as the boss affect your members' drive, you should always know how these impact them. Never forget that team spirit stands as the company's soul. As such, you should always ensure your subordinates enjoy doing their duties being a team member to make them an essential portion of the company's plans.

Now, how do you do this? Foremost of all, you will need to take your subordinates' place and see things from their angle. This is where empathy plays a salient role in making your staff emotionally and mentally more robust, especially during tough times. Bear in mind that accomplishing a challenging job carrying a great weight inculcates a feeling of success among employees.

Thus, you must make your people feel that they are doing a vital function indispensable for the company's success and well-being as a whole. This motivational feature drives people to fulfill targets, and more so when you are also self-motivated. This means you know yourself, your needs, besides having a strong desire to do everything within your power to meet your goals.

Only when you are driven yourself can you be a role model for others to follow and motivate others. The primary motivation techniques are extrinsic and intrinsic. Extrinsic motivation is when you do things out of necessity, such as your need for money. This means that you are left with no choice but to simply do it to survive.

In contrast, intrinsic motivation is when you do things because you just love doing them. In your career and entire life, you'll come across folks who are moved by any of these factors, but most often through a blend of these two motivation types. Still, take note that people's motivations change at certain times, as well as for different jobs.

To manage or lead people well, you must know the balance amid their drive. This knowledge can also be used when rewarding different people, such as providing some people with trickier duties as a reward. In contrast, others may get an additional day off with pay. Now, if you are running out of creativity in your style of motivating your people at the workplace, here are some suggestions you may still have not tried:

1. Allowing members autonomy in solving personal problems instead of meddling;
2. Asking for recommendations regarding departmental goals;
3. Coaching new workers in a supportive and engaging manner;

4. Giving a pay raise or bonus based on output to team members meeting the proper outcomes;
5. Handing out professional development sources to your most motivated workers;
6. Passing on desired tasks to highly engaged staff;

7. Carrying out team building workshops every three months to increase teamwork and mutual respect;
8. Checking the distinct growth of staff in taking on more tasks;
9. Focus on prospects towards boosting staff engagement, accountability, and retention;
10. Giving the staff the power to select the way they can address goals when given a chance;
11. Looking at your own work and interaction style to find better ways of inspiring others and being a role model;
12. Noting the inputs of the team, besides showing pleasure, at all times;
13. Talking over staff concerns in a helpful way devoid of any judgment;
14. Helping to improve relations across management and staff levels to perk up connection, foster teamwork, and put up a shared feeling of mission;
15. Finding and being grateful for the unique inputs and talents of members of a team;

16. Putting up an open tally board towards logging matching sales by various sales team members;
17. Joining casual staff chats during their work break to mingle and gain an insight into their traits and concerns;
18. Keenly weighing up staff matters in various projects and tasks;
19. Launching free wellness and health programs;
20. Keeping a tight rein on staff meeting periods by staying on a strict outline and wrapping up talks quickly;
21. Looking at ways to gain knowledge from mistakes rather than imposing penalties;
22. Meeting up with an assistant to set working goals;
23. Mentioning positive facets of the leadership or management approach of your supervisor to her boss at a casual gathering;
24. Preparing a budget request for additional personnel to directors that emphasizes the way revenues will be enhanced;
25. Proposing to support coworkers who are dealing with stuff that causes anxiety;
26. Providing personal testimonials to potential recipients at a seminar of an organization that grants funding;
27. Recognizing the inputs of crucial givers in press releases;
28. Sending a commendation note to the supervisor of another team after getting the help needed by your team;
29. Spotting and quietly expressing thanks to peers for voluntary acts of project or work initiative, as well as interpersonal kindness;
30. Taking to lunch a solid departmental contributor as an act of gratitude for his support;
31. Thanking your immediate supervisor for his backing;
32. Utilizing new technologies to make work processes more efficient and straightforward, besides reducing caseloads;
33. Warning an assistant of the effects of consistently being late when reporting for work;

34. Writing a recommendation on LinkedIn for a supportive business partner; or,
35. Yielding ownership and control of different project phases to teammates who merit the chance to lead other workers.

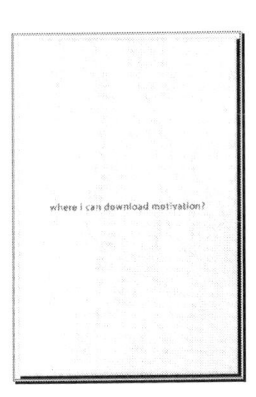

where i can download motivation?

Indeed, motivation exists as an essential competence that can give you positive outcomes, irrespective of being a manager or leader. If motivating other people is among your key fortes, then this stays as a flair that you wish your employers know because it can cause your growth and the firm.

We will be talking next about a good manager's secrets other than those we have already discussed.

Chapter 4: What Makes a Good Manager?

A wholesome manager puts himself as an upbeat model and fathoms how to use his strengths to inspire his team to do well. Fruitful managers function along with their staff and colleagues to build a complete work setting. As mentioned in the previous chapters, to be good at handling people, it is vital to pass on targets, hopes, and advice.

Meanwhile, business demands, irrespective of size, are shifting at the pace of technology, needs of the time, and increased scope. Above all, businesses need people, especially managers, who possess specific traits on top of evolving skills and sentience that are often not easily measurable.

Commercial Awareness

Also known as business acumen or shrewdness, this refers to insight into what accounts for a firm's success. This can rope in the selling or buying of items or sourcing services for a given market. It's crucial for you, as a manager, to acquire this kind of insight to fully detect strengths and weak spots within teams besides the business as a whole.

Vital business insight within management may be what divides failure and triumph in today's trade climate. Hence, management training programs these days add in essential business skills. Examples include customer service, sales, relationship management, as well as negotiation tactics.

Sadly, learning management in schools often fails to include teaching business skills in an ample volume. Thus, in essence, this causes a skill chasm within the workers of today. Taking no notice of business skills training for managers can miss a growth area giving rise to a big trade lead above rivals. By setting goals that need management to perk up their business acumen, primarily within managers, they are far likely to struggle to meet their targets. This can be as easy as reshuffling a team, if not retrain managers, to make sure that their strengths are utilized for commercial triumph and weaknesses used by way of a basis to learn and get better.

Uses and benefits

Many companies view commercial awareness by way of a critical need in potential managers. People who devote time to figure out how the company operates and earns, besides how the trade works as a group, are the kind of persons who demonstrate an elevated level of interest, motivation, and effort on the outcome.

Thus, this awareness facilitates new managers to rev up and make primed decisions right before taking office. Also, commercial awareness improves your performance as a manager. When you work out the industry you are working in and see how your job helps your company compete, you end up:

1. Boosting your odds of promotion,
2. Building your standing as a skilled manager stronger,
3. Dealing with risks well,
4. Getting reasonable rates and terms from suppliers, and
5. Increasing your chances of meeting clients' needs.

Whatever industry you're working in, commercial insight is helpful. In fact, even managers in the government and nonprofit organizations will gain much from developing it. Come to think of it, commercial awareness is a crucial advantage when you wish to rise up the ladder in these areas.

Forward Planning

This is a practice geared to the future that involves finding the viable plan or vision for a section in the firm and then listing the actions and the changes required towards making the program happen. This means thinking of future settings or needs each time you create a plan.

In a commercial environment, it stays as a scheme that relates to the company's long-term prospects. So, it considers possibilities of development, uncertainties, and likely downfalls that can obstruct the business's success. With this skill, minimizing future delays from occurring in the company's operation is among its goals.

A sample of this is a small firm forward planning for a slump and getting ready ahead of time to ensure that the business will not go bankrupt. As a manager with plenty of skills that include forward planning, you can help the firm reap its gains, as follows:

Increase morale for both employees and employer

Anything can occur to a firm that could mess up operations. The perfect example is what is happening to the business world today due to the pandemic. Another example is a natural calamity, like super hurricanes, that can disturb business operations and the safety of people, family, and properties.

With existing forward planning, any firm can set up an emergency plan and budget to ensure a quick upturn. As a result, this will increase the workers' morale as they know that the firm cares about them and their future.

Secure and egg on wise spending within the firm

Among the most central things that a small firm needs to consider consist of business operations and income. If there remain noticeable declines in the financial gain, this will impact the employees, besides the entire firm. A deficiency in regulation within the company can cause dissatisfied customers, lost products, and poor internal and quality control.

Any business obstacle that might emerge will not affect the financial gain a lot when forward planning occurs. Now, how is this possible? If the business stands stable and avoids wasting resources, it can save up enough resources for the rainy days. Also, through forward planning, maximizing resources is ensure that results in better customer relations and satisfaction, as well as fulfilling business targets efficiently.

Interpersonal Skills

Also termed as people skills, these are soft skills needing EI to exchange ideas with others. These skills build trust that is crucial between managers and team members. These skills also help you be productive at work, make positive and strong relationships with colleagues, and facilitate the smooth and practical completion of team projects.

Technically speaking, these are tools managers and people generally use to relate and interact with others in a working environment. These skills, therefore, can impact the drive and output of an entire team, department, and company. Other than those we have previously discussed, there are still more focal interpersonal skills needed by managers.

Negotiation

Within a work milieu, negotiation means forming an accord among at least two parties that each party finds good enough. These parties can be office workers, business owners or bosses, colleagues, or outside persons. This mainly involves finding the middle ground among parties.

Take note, though, that parleyed contracts do not necessarily involve parties equally meeting halfway because one party might have more influence than the other party. Negotiations might give rise to contracts or formal agreements. In some cases, though, it may produce a mere verbal agreement or any other less formal deal of the manner of remedying a problem, if not determining the route of action.

Negotiation exists as a vital flair for many management positions. Subject to the specific role in a company, it might also involve creating contracts between service providers and clients or assisting colleagues in resolving a problem to determine a way out. To become good at negotiating, you must know how to actively listen to all parties concerned. From the info gathered, you must use problem-solving skills to reach a conclusion that satisfies all parties.

Assertiveness

To successfully manage your people, your team members have to respect and follow you. And this is where assertiveness enters the picture. Bear in mind that your prime task is to complete your work through your members while simultaneously ensuring that their morale is at a reasonable level.

On top of this, it is also your responsibility to keep them driven to reach the target goals. It is sad to note that managers find it challenging to locate their place within a department. The main reason for this is their not wanting to be seen by way of a micromanager. And, of course, they also do not wish to be thought an easy prey.

So, this is the perennial challenge all managers have no choice but to face. In reality, a good manager is assertive but fair. Thus, managers' assertiveness means urging other people to be honest and open about their viewpoints, wishes, and sentiments. This is important in the workplace as it can make both the manager and staff act appropriately.

Patience

Also a virtue and actually among leaders' core qualities, patience is the power to accept, if not tolerate delay, nuisance, or suffering devoid of anger or getting upset. As a skill, you can always boost this gift and take part in drills to become more patient. As a rule, being patient can give rise to more realistic prospects and overall calm behavior.

Most people believe this denotes maturity, perhaps because we tend to be more patient as we grow old. Yet, most people do not know that patience fosters a steady identity across time and eggs on people to take on responsibilities. Patience, an essential attribute of a leader, also demands flairs more often linked to management.

After all, your ability to manage people patiently requires you to tackle situations wherein you may find yourself. This means that you have to understand the setting and confirm the facts. For this reason, a patient manager never fails to understand any situation. He can quickly assess how critical the problem is and its resolution.

So, as a manager, you must support your skills, besides that of your people, to gain knowledge of the setting you face. Also, patience is needed when creating plans. Tolerance demands that you must know whatever you are planning to do. And planning exists among the critical management work that enables you to build confidence from the people you work with.

In the process, it builds and gets the needed support. Any good manager is aware that the most pleasing way to boot out impatient business owners' demands is by possessing an engaged and powerful boss. So, enlist and retain the proper backing because it is a vital component to managing patiently.

Also, you need to execute your program as scheduled. Having the trust to follow your plan stays challenging. Still, stand your ground even when other people attack you. Besides, ensure you do your best to meet commitments. Finally, be ready to act on unexpected events.

Remember, most plans always hit a dead end at specific points or derail due to unplanned events. Thus, a good program will stay as-is when a great manager holds the knack to respond well even when things turn awry. Unforeseen occasions are the constant ordeal of patience; therefore, you must prepare plans that will help you react accordingly.

Conflict management

Likewise known as conflict resolution, this involves designing an office that precludes discord, besides a manager or team that handles and works out workplace issues well. Strong skills in this area are a plus in most posts, as the conflict remains virtually hopeless to avoid.

To disagree is part of our humanity, and disagreements stand healthy when tackled correctly. In fact, eliminating conflict lock, stock, and barrel can also cause its unique problems. These may come in the absence of diverse opinions in the workplace or no means for managers to spot and correct weak programs, systems, and policies.

It really does not matter whatever position you may have. Whatever post you hold, you will most likely have to resolve clashes one day in your career. This might consist of solving a problem between two team members. It can also be a disagreement between you and a coworker.

In certain situations, it can be a dispute between your company and a client or supplier. And just like when you are negotiating, you will have to actively and fairly listen to both parties. And, obviously, you will have to use your creativity and problem-solving skills to get a solution.

Without a ready conflict management approach for your office, two persons with unlike mindsets may find it hard to work together under pressure. That is why it is needed for both managers and staff to know the typical manner conflicts are handled in the workplace and how conflict resolution methods are implemented.

Actually, there are different techniques people generally use when facing a conflict. These are avoidance, competition, change, compromise, and group effort. The mode you handle fights may feel wholly customary to you, although foreign to someone else. So, if you ask me, the ideal solution is collaboration. Being a manager, managing work and people with unique personalities is your daily ritual. Sometimes, strong traits can cause tension that affects work success in the long run. Therefore, it's in the best interest of everyone to handle conflict well at the workplace.

Mentoring

This exists as a learning rapport, generally engrossed in long-term career growth. Its primary reason is to drive individual growth through building skills, wisdom, and understanding. Generally, your boss seems to be the perfect guru to lead you across the next stage of your job.

As your director, this person sees firsthand your strong points, abilities, and goals. What is more, he can offer you feedback, besides guidance, that is precise to your position and career route. After decades of research on this topic, the proof is irrefutable. It is now an accepted fact that people who possess strong mentors build up a horde of professional gains, including:

1. A more robust identity,
2. Better organizational commitment,
3. Extreme job satisfaction,
4. Faster advancement in the corporate ladder, and
5. Higher salaries.

We will keep this topic short and sweet as we will take this up again in the last chapter of this book.

Organization

This group focuses on skills that are linked to making systems and order, besides lifting output levels. It also entails ranking tasks that need the soonest completion against work that could be postponed, passed on to another worker, or entirely done away with. Having solid skills in this area can bring down the odds of taking in poor work routines, such as putting off work or messing up the work area. It can also include failure to clearly and thoroughly communicate and adopting a wasteful behavior. This skill is split into groups, as follows:

External

Under this group, work projects remain typically centered over a rigid outline, and breaking work into smaller tasks and goals as an effective means of completing them. Naturally, employers prefer workers who schedule and can delegate smaller tasks among a team. This assures them that workers correctly stay on the right track with cut-off dates while keeping up a wholesome balance amid work and personal life.

Internal

These skills encompass simply maintaining a clutter-free work desk. While keeping a clear area to work exists important, neatness stays just one of the many vital skills. Workers with excellent skills in this area also keep themselves tranquil and ready with systematic working out and scheduling.

Physical

This group includes a tidy work table, layout of floors, rooms, the whole office buildings, and well beyond looking after a neat look. A poorly arranged space causes physical discomfort and even lost time, objects, and people. It is a fact that the area we work in shows a lot about how well we perform. Thus, you, as the manager, must help design the workspaces for everyone to maintain order.

Problem-solving

Now, let us add more to what we have discussed on problem-solving skills. At this point, I believe we all agree that acquiring this skill can help us solve issues fast and effectively. It is among the key competencies that employers look for in candidates for managerial positions.

And why is this so? The answer is quite simple. People with problem-solving skills are primarily self-reliant. After all, this skill requires quickly finding the underlying issues and carrying out a solution. It is actually a soft skill or a solid personal trait because it is learned through training, education, or work experience.

You can even improve your skills in this area by acquainting yourself with shared industry issues and gaining knowledge from experienced managers. Let's now look at the steps typically employed in problem-solving.

Probing contributing factors

To figure out a problem, the first thing you must know is what set it off. This calls for gathering and evaluating data, isolate likely contributing conditions, and pinpointing what has to be tackled for a solution. To fix this, you will have to use data gathering and analysis skills, fact-finding, and historical research.

Making interventions

Once you find out the source, brainstorm possible actions to take to resolve the problem. Sometimes, this draws in teamwork since the more people working things out, the more valuable and creative the input is. A single approach is seldom the apparent path to solving complex problems.

Thus, coming up with a cluster of options facilitates covering your bases and reducing your danger of letdown should the initial strategy implemented fails. This involves brainstorming, thinking out of the box, prediction, forecasting, and project design with planning.

Evaluating strategies

Subject to the problem's nature and your firm's pecking order, gauging best lines of attack may be done by the assigned groups, team managers, or sent to the business chief. The person or group who gets to decide must assess likely costs, required assets, and possible stumbling blocks to fruitful carrying out the action plan. This calls for some skills plus probing, talking things over, a solid joint effort, testing stage, mediation, and ranking.

Carrying out the approved action plan

When the proposed plan has been approved, it is time to implement it with standards that can swiftly and accurately determine if the program is working. This putting into practice also involves announcing the changes in the SOPs or standard operating procedures to the personnel. Skills required here include project management and implementation, collaboration, benchmark development, and time management.

Assessing the effectiveness of the solution

Upon carrying out the approved plan, the best solvers of problems have installed systems to assess its use, besides how quickly it works. In this manner, they make out right away if the problem has been solved or if they have to tweak their response towards the problem without delay. This demands informing all people concerned, analyzing data, doing surveys, getting feedback from clients or staff, following through the process, and damage control.

Strategic thinking

This stays as a crucial skill for many jobs, chiefly business developers, management consultants, besides strategic cost and operations experts. Strategic planning exists as the system of setting up a company vision and making that vision happen through small, doable goals.

Workers involved in this area help set targets, decide what workers have to do, and help them achieve those targets. Of course, every job will need various work experiences and skills! Some types of skills under this group are as follows:

Analytical

People taking on strategic planning tasks need to know how to test and assess a firm's business plan. They ought to be experts in analyzing the market and feasibility studies, among many others. Only with an analytic eye can these planners decide on what a firm has to take on.

In so doing, they should be skilled in paying attention to details; computing the cost of carrying out plans and projects; critical, systematic, and logical thinkers; defining input mechanisms and the rationale behind the process of strategic planning; developing a program for implementing schemes; and, excellent in inductive and deductive reasoning.

Decisive

Since strategic planning entails many instances linked to options or choices, the planners have to select an action plan. In this way, they can help a business attain its goals free of overthinking and constant doubts. They need to examine every available information to confidently come up with a thoughtful choice. This calls for them to be very good at delegating, assigning heads, and building consensus. On top of that, they should excel in fixing measurable goals, creating and carrying out timelines, prioritizing, and are goal-oriented and confident.

everything is connected

I believe you now have a clear picture of what a good manager is. In the next chapter, we will look into the top qualities of a leader.

Chapter 5: Qualities of a Leaders

Everyone holds the potential to become a leader. Still, only a few choose to become one and aim for a certain level of greatness. It does not matter if you have successfully worked up the company ladder through hard work or just launched your own firm. Whichever way, the route towards leadership is certainly not an effortless one. Along the way, you have or will encounter assorted types of circumstances and emotions.

You will go through good times, demanding ones, and a sprinkle of terrible periods. Despite the stressful times faced, a splendid leader can always lead his people to success. To properly help you get better results in your career and boost your leadership style, some essential qualities must be developed and learned. For entrepreneurs, on the other hand, making sure that your company is guided by a strong leader possessing the right skills is key to your success.

Without a rich vision directed by a strong leader who monitors your business, you are sadly not in the offing to get your dreams and aspirations to become a reality. At this point, it would be helpful to see if your senior company officers already possess the featured natural leadership assets that we shall discuss in this chapter.

Commitment

Nothing shows this quality until you buckle down with your employees. There exists no more superb drive than seeing leaders working alongside everybody else. By showing your commitment towards your team and company, you'll not only get their respect but will likewise instill that same diligent drive amid your staff. Baring your sense of commitment lays down the model for other people to follow. Just in case you do not know it yet, this simple act leads to better loyalty and high opinion for you being a leader. So, set the commitment tone for others to follow.

Remember, if you assume that your team will work hard to produce excellent work, you need to guide them by being an example. Commitment exists as a leadership trait that inspires and catches the fancy of the people as a whole. It reveals that the leading light has convictions, besides believing in the vision.

I assure you, the team will first have to believe in their leader ahead of accepting the vision set. As such, we can safely say that commitment stays as an issue of the heart, which is essential in leadership. Why? Have you observed how people work together at a greater level once the commitment is shared?

Commitment fosters friendship, trust, and kindness. These are what a group requires to keep things going for a long time. Suppose people remain committed towards an effort covering some time. In that case, they'll learn whatever they have to know towards becoming more effective. For leaders to practice commitment, they need to base it on their primary work.

Modeling the way

To do this, you need to find your tone by making your personal values clear. From there, you can set yourself as a benchmark by aligning your actions with mutual values. After all, you need to practice whatever you preach and get to reap whatever you sow for others to follow.

The bottom line is that anything you do will return to you. If you live in a glasshouse, never throw stones. And you know what? All leaders stand for the values they cherish, for only then can they find their unique voice. Therefore, setting yourself as the suitable model for your team to behave and perform is crucial.

As a leader, all eyes stay naturally on you. For example, if you come to work on time and are smartly dressed, people will eventually grasp that you expect them to do the same. When you start rolling up your shirt sleeves and get to work, they will know that you mean business.

They would be ashamed if they do not do their part in achieving company goals. When they observe how you communicate to somebody higher than you on the corporate ladder, they will understand your accountability when things exist going badly. Anyone who sees how professional a team member is in his dealings will immediately conclude that his boss must be very professional in his dealings, as well. If you fail in leading by example, you may find it very challenging to guide your people to the correct behavior or performance level.

Inspiring a common vision

As a leader, have you envisioned the future through imagining moving and ennobling actions? You can actually do this when you enlist other people in a shared vision by drawing mutual aspirations. You can also create a broad picture to avoid the "scarcity mentality," which seems to be the standard conditioning of corporate workers.

In psychology, this mentality is used to describe people who see life by way of a fixed pie that if someone takes a huge slice, the rest will have to settle for smaller portions. In its place, support the abundance mentality, which believes that there is enough of everything for everyone.

As Stephen Covey explained, the solution remains to frame out a larger space where all get to take a share and use to their advantage the limitless opportunities on hand in work and life.

Challenging the course of action

Only when you question the process can you search for chances of coming up with innovative means to change, nurture and improve. This entails experimenting and taking risks by constantly generating small triumphs and finding the gems of wisdom in the wrong choices. In the process, you are continuously practicing progress, which the Japanese call the Kaizen mindset. This can be likened to Stephen Covey's proactivity. In this mindset, people are encouraged not to react to a situation by criticizing or finding faults.

Instead, react proactively by finding solutions or suggesting improvement. In this journey, you will need to focus on slight, incremental improvements and build drive from small victories. Remember the last time you rolled snowballs down a hill? You started with a small ball, right? When it started rolling down, it slowly grew more prominent. And that applies to success, as well. Hence, a leader continuously develops his skills.

Empowering others to take action

A good leader fosters collaboration by helping attain collective goals while building trust. He strengthens other people by sharing command and discretion. In lifting others up, he helps them find their own unique voice and the best in them. By leveraging the distinctive values that other people possess, great leaders are unleashing a person's leadership qualities.

You are actually liberating your people to employ their own abilities. And this happens when you make them feel that they are doing their part in making the shared vision come true. So, you must acknowledge the strengths and contributions your people have. When you do this, you are already inviting them to become leaders and chip in their power to the common cause.

Empowerment is the means leaders use to involve their teams in making decisions. This gives members active participation that makes the most of their own judgment and expertise. As a result, this increases the members' sense of commitment towards the organization and individual worth.

Encouraging the heart

Good leaders always recognize the contributions of their team by giving a positive reception for their individual excellence. It can be in the form of a simple smile, greeting, or asking the staff his opinion and listening. Any action that sincerely tells your team members that you genuinely care is already encouraging their hearts.

Hence, you must stay objective and open-minded to become a caring leader who celebrates your team's victories and values. In the process, you are already creating a sense of community. Always bear in mind that when you encourage people, they feel influential and respected.

These feelings never fail to bring out the finest in people. Thus, when you do this, you are adding value by being confident of your team's potential. Coupled with providing resources to facilitate your people to achieve better outcomes, you live with passion linked to results. So, do not be stingy in celebrating small wins and giving rewards to your people's excellent performance.

Creativity

You are a good lead when your team members consult you for solutions to predicaments or answers to puzzling questions at work. This happens when they see you thinking out of the box, as shown by your actions each time an issue arises. Another thing that triggers them to run to you is when they see that you have the habit of gathering the team to start brainstorming viewpoints to build your ideas from.

Creativity is an essential leadership quality because it is vital in making decisions for various reasons. Through this quality, you can further encourage the heart of your people. On top of that, your ability to weigh up things both logically and innovatively will help you produce more balanced business outcomes.

When you lead creatively, you are driving productivity further and fostering success in the company. After all, creativity gives leaders the gift to go into new ways to solve problems that others do not readily see. Hence, creativity exists as a critical skill for leaders because if they do not harness new viewpoints, they will stagnate.

Let's face it. To properly achieve creative transformation, we need to mess up a bit how things stand, right? And this is in line with the leader's role of challenging the process, which leads to doing things differently, besides breaking free from what is usual to the business.

Feedback

If you wish to boost your leadership further, you definitely need to receive and give feedback. It is critical in leadership positions because it allows the managers and supervisors to identify likely conflicts between employees, if not conflict that the leader may have with them.

Encouraging feedback aids team members to open up, as well as voice their views about the way you are leading them. It allows them to convey whatever works better for them, besides what is not working, in your leadership style. If you wish to get feedback that's necessary for improving your leadership style, you may consider the following suggestions:

1. Ask feedback deftly;
2. Build and uphold a mentally safe environment;
3. Request both negative and positive information;
4. When getting feedback, pay full attention, as well as listen carefully.

Flexibility

You are flexible as a leader when you can modify your style or attitude to leadership when responding to unpredictable circumstances. Also, flexible leaders adapt to variations as they arise. They can brush up their plans towards incorporating new innovations to overcome challenges and still achieve goals.

Everybody knows that change exists unavoidable and almost always happens when you least expect it. For this reason, all nations' leaders face constant variations and complexity consisting of evolving cultures, jobs, markets, and competition. Thus, to prosper, a leader must have the ability to adjust to these shifts and new conditions.

This calls for adaptive leadership where the leader sees change, not in the form of a blockage, but a chance to getting ready for a possible opportunity. Let us now dive into the three key behaviors that help people of all ranks to accept a leadership type that is adaptive in navigating changes more quickly.

Flexible thinking

Having an adaptive cognitive approach permits leaders to employ different thinking schemes and mental contexts. Deepening perspective and awareness help leaders know how they process ideas, their mode of thinking, and their customers' way of weighing things up. Some fundamental actions you may consider to practice unlocking flexibility in your thoughts are:

1. Examining how flexible your emotions are by reflecting on them with those of other people. Then, honestly assessing if you can vary your style in dealing with the feelings of other people.

2. Relaxing your mind to grant yourself the ease of stepping back from stringent processes and logical thinking. In doing so, you allow yourself to fool around with the thought of a novel paradigm.

3. Questioning your thinking patterns to be sure that you are moving toward issues with a free mind and exploring them from all levels.

Planning ahead

Adaptable leaders know that, though a goal and vision are needed, the route towards them has to be open. When you practice an adaptive style of leading people, you make multiple plans to reach your goals. Instead of sticking to one solution for solving a problem, you have contingency plans ready just in case the first plan fails to work.

And with planning, you are allowing appropriate reactions to the need of the times, besides creating a focus on your available resources and your people's energy to reach goals. What is more, planning helps you to assess dangers and opportunities by providing a platform to check them out in the current situation, as well as possible upcoming events. By sensing the obstacles you may face with the full knowledge of available tools, you can lessen the risk while maximizing the reward.

Curiosity

This trait helps to free the mind, makes growth possible, encourages new beliefs, and stays as a fundamental standard of flexible leadership. Curiosity generates queries that exercise problem-solving skills to find results. If you wish to further develop this trait, start asking questions, paying attention to the answers given to you, and observing the process.

It is crucial, though, that you must first seek to understand what the other person is saying and refrain from explaining your point of view. You must wonder, explore, as well as consider other people's viewpoints before judging or deciding. Thus, it is of utmost essence that you understand others' perspectives and be willing to listen in ambiguity, openness, and curiosity without being so concerned with the outcome.

After all, as a leader, you must develop the flair to uncover, besides checking values, assumptions, and beliefs. So, be curious about others' opinions, perspectives, as well as approaches. Remember, everyone tackles things differently; hence, potential answers or solutions to setbacks can be veiled by how other people weigh things up.

Also, thinking out of the box helps a lot in developing your curiosity. As a rule, leaders are aware of building a growth mentality that creates space for novelty and continuous gaining of knowledge. In the process, they make a safe setting for risk-taking using new models, besides fast failures, towards accelerating learning.

To adapt, you have to experiment, right? And the reason behind this is because no one is born with an adaptable attitude. With training and focus, you can develop the traits needed to lead people flexibly that helps foster navigation over the path of a changing landscape.

Positivity

Being optimistic takes commitment and a lot of work. When you remain positive, you'll find it stress-free to create a system of supporters and members who always stand ready to lend a hand when needed. Thus, positive leaders stand more effective when leading successful teams and projects while creating a positive ethos.

Needless to say, positivity paves the way to success primarily because of the psychological benefits it offers. Have you observed that optimistic people are more energetic, self-confident, not easily discouraged, and hopeful? Yes, they are because their positivity tends to drive them to set higher targets and take the extra mile to properly reach their targets. It also helps them to see many solutions to setbacks and make excellent decisions. To raise your people's positive traits, you must seek to fashion a workplace that promotes more connection and work production among them.

> FORGIVE THE NEGATIVE PEOPLE, THEY LEARNED TO MANY LIES.
> —Lil B

By displaying passion and confidence as a leader, you can understand its effect on a working environment. Obviously, holding on to a positive feeling is not always possible, especially when you have to tackle every task each day as a leader. Still, the more pessimism you can stop from influencing your workers, the more possible it is for you to have positive results.

All things considered, you need to sustain your team's motivation for your company's continued achievement. So, you really have to keep their energy levels at a high level, right? It is a relief that you can do this through many ways, such as providing coffee, snacks, relationship advice, and an occasional team dinner in a nearby restaurant.

Suppose you always bear in mind that each team member is a human being. In that case, you can find many other ways to keep the office's mood a fine blend of productivity and good humor. Rest assured that if your people are in high spirits and feeling upbeat, there's a big chance that they would gladly stay for 60 minutes more to complete a report. If not, they would happily devote their most outstanding abilities to work for the company.

Responsibility

Have you come across a leader who does not take responsibility for the whole team's performance? Well, if you had, then that person is not a good leader! Leaders often praise the workers when things go as planned. When problems happen, though, they see them quickly, find solutions, and guide the team in the right direction.

And that is because responsible leadership stays all about making workable business decisions that take account of everyone's welfare. This includes all shareholders, the community, employees, customers, suppliers, the environment, besides future generations. Thus, great leaders understand that they have to take responsibility for not succeeding as far as the company is concerned.

This responsibility means they cannot make excuses. The only recourse for them in the face of failure is to accept the fault and then find ways to resolve the problem at the soonest possible time. And for this reason, responsibility is beyond doubt a key attribute. In line with this, leaders must be:

Ready to seek and accept accountability for your decisions and actions

Leaders play a salient role in guiding and inspiring their people while finding ways to get the business moving towards new heights. Naturally, when things are not going right, it is also their responsibility to determine why things are off track. Upon identifying the possible causes, they have to take remedial and decisive actions.

In the process, you have to keep your team informed. Once again, allow me to reiterate, strong communication stays as a critical skill required in leaders. In fact, a leader cannot take on his responsibilities without this skill. In their varied forms, excellent communication skills are needed for a leader to be a role model to his people. It is also required when ensuring long-term company success and in improving the work performance of workers.

Technically proficient

You ought to stay a rung ahead of the team, especially in technology impacting your company. So, it really would help if you subscribe to websites featuring industry blogs. You may also read papers that can help you keep updated with technological innovations in your business sector.

You are not expected to be skilled at everything. Yet, you should at least understand the risks and opportunities your company may face due to technological innovations. In this way, you can make timely and sound decisions, which is vital for all leaders. By making sure that you are fast in solving problems and making decisions, it would be helpful to use the latest planning tools and devices that can strengthen your leadership.

Trustworthiness

If you have this quality as a leader, it is easy for you to see and believe in your people's best traits. You do your work as a leader on the principle that most workers want to perform excellently. As a result, your people find you approachable and respectable. And this is especially true when you openly show your accountability on their performance and behavior at work. Since you are mutually helpful to everyone devoid of discrimination, it is natural for your people to trust you. As a result, the commitment of your people to team objectives is increased.

This leads to a workplace atmosphere where communication is improved, and ideas are shared more freely; thus, increasing the team's productivity and creativity. Most importantly, employees are further comfortable with variations and more ready to accept a new idea when led by a trusted leader.

Take note, though, that trust is something that cannot be commanded to anyone, nor does it go with a company position. If you wish your team to have faith in you, you must earn it. So, how can you get your people to trust you? Perhaps, the best way is for you to consistently employ these qualities.

Similarity or Congruity

As a leader, your beliefs and values are apparent and match everything you do and say. Come what may, you always behave and interact with people as you believe fitting. And this congruity earns other people's trust. After all, leadership concerns doing good things that are often not so easy to do.

And, as far as leaders are concerned, standing for what they believe in is the right thing to do. Come to think of it, when you simply take the easiest path because you fear a negative response from people, then you do not really support your beliefs. If this is the case, how can you expect others to trust you?

The answer is quite simple. You must make sure that what you say and do aligns with your values. Otherwise, you are breeding doubts and making it hard for your people to have faith in you.

Constancy

We have talked a lot about vision as a requirement for leadership. And this vision looks beyond current reality that propels us to work towards making it come true. I know it may sometimes require you to make an impossible dream possible. Still, a vision by itself does not produce trust.

And that is where constancy enters the picture. This denotes that you must stay on the course towards the vision, which takes guts. This is especially true when you are surrounded by cynics. Perhaps, this is why Henry George Bohn said that boldness is the main thing as far as business is concerned.

In due course, your consistency to your vision will get other people's trust, besides motivating them. After all, if your behavior can inspire other people to dream, learn, do, and become a better person, you are indeed a leader.

Integrity or Honesty

Now, tell me, is this an easy one? Yes, it means you are the type of person who keeps your promises. As such, people value your word as a valuable promise that never fails. This is important because leaders' capacity to implement change is vital in the same way as their capacity to cling to what is good.

Thus, you should hold fast on doing whatever you said you'll do. Perhaps, this is why people look for credibility from their leaders. And when we talk of credibility, nothing can build it up or shoot it down quicker than honoring or breaking your promises.

Dependability or Reliability

Finally, you know that you are building trust once your workers know you are always there when they need you. You strengthen them in their moments of weakness. You present yourself as a reliable guide, source of inspiration, mentor, and coworker, not as a fair-weather buddy who forgets about you when someone better comes along.

Actually, the importance of reliability is felt most during the small moments in a person's life. Although your character can also be revealed in life's beautiful moments, it is honed in the tiny instances. And when there is any question concerning someone's dependability, it always brings down the degree of trust in that person.

These qualities exist as the base of good leadership. Although some traits are more naturally found in the leader's personality, it is certainly something anyone can develop, besides strengthen with time. Next, we will talk about how you can unleash the leader in you. For now, let me end this chapter with a reminder. Managers may take on the challenge of persuading workers to do stuff commonly not preferred to do. Still, the task of inspiring workers to do things they never even dreamed they could do belongs to leaders.

Chapter 6: Unleashing the Leader in You

I firmly believe that there is a natural leader in each person in this world. Our individual inner leader exists as a powerful spring that gives us confidence and guides us during uncertain times. It holds the wisdom behind the choices we make and prompts us to look for help when direly needed. Most of all, this tiny seed of leadership identifies our available sources to grow as a person that we may eventually steer others to develop.

This leader in us gives us clarity to pinpoint what we truly want. It also helps propel us forward in our personal and professional life. As each of us is born unique into this world, bringing out that leader in us may require distinctive ways. The proper way always starts with a strong desire to turn ourselves into a mighty leader that people will follow, respect, and admire.

This desire will give us the strength and courage to take on the journey of unleashing the leader in us. Unique as you are, your process is equally striking. So, feel free to choose from the listed suggestions coming in next on what's best for you to do. I'm sure that the leader in you will give you the hints you need.

Believe in Yourself

Irrespective of what other people may say, nothing changes the fact that you matter. Otherwise, why would they even bother to put you down? This stays as a critical step in unleashing the leader in you. Everything starts from within. When you knock into the focal point of yourself, you are knocking into a formidable guidance structure that fires you up like nothing can ever do. You are given the power to line up your core gifts with whatever you do to set that meaningful goal of bringing your unique worth upfront and in focus. Upon remembering that you matter, you are actually being energized to the point of making it possible for you to inspire others, as well.

Shed Off Wishful Thinking

Have you observed that wishful thinking always starts with the word "should?" This term is among the dodgiest words in your inner dialogue because it shows that you are trying to meet others' expectations or opinions. An example is:

"I should have just continued working even when I was really exhausted. Had I done that, I may have met my deadline."

Given the example, so you did not meet your deadline because you slept. The questions are: What is it that you truly desire? What is more important to you? What inspires you? Obviously, the goal here is to produce quality work that meets the deadline without sacrificing your health.

Instead of spending time on wishful thinking, reprogram your thoughts. Set yourself free from that image of perfection and settle in your own self. In its place, learn from the experience and nurture yourself realistically. Be grateful for what life is giving you at the moment.

Accept Responsibility

You fashion your world around the decisions you make based on your available choices or options. So, take full accountability for your reality and carry out building from it. Whatever your present circumstances are, you always have the choice. Will you sit back watching what life throws your way?

Or, will you start making personal choices in your life? When you opt to be the driver of your life, circumstances beyond your control will no longer have much influence over you.

Know Yourself

At this point, can you identify your core beliefs? Do you know what inspires you and furnishes you that sense of commitment? Are you aware of your core nature and unique gifts, besides weak points? If your answers are all affirmative, what stops you from bringing them forward in your everyday life?

You can always start by finding ways to line them up with your work. If whatever you do is not allied to your values, perhaps, you need to devote some time to discern what kind of work can help bring out the best in you.

Accept All of You

You cannot do this until you know your strengths, weaknesses, and everything else that comprises your entire self. With such knowledge, you can choose to change yourself by strengthen your assets, working on your weak points, and continually pushing yourself towards a higher level.

Only when you can accept yourself hook, line, and sinker can you start liking and loving yourself. You must feel comfortable with yourself because, if not, it will be difficult for you to make realistic decisions that work well for you. Perhaps, you can start with being mindful of your true self while seeking to be better each day.

In everything you do, see the reasons why you are doing them. For example, assess if your habits are in line with your goal of self-improvement. Also, take the time to discern the knowledge you gain in reading books and various content circulated on the web. Are they in line with or challenge your core values?

Take on Challenges Life Brings Along the Way

Instead of spending a lifetime struggling over each roadblock, how about embracing them? With the right mindset, you can shift how you see the challenges that life brings into your daily life. And when you have succeeded, you will realize that they are actually opportunities for you to grow.

In reality, each challenge exists as a chance to learn. It can also serve as a test on what you already knew. It can be something new or anything that validates something related to your field of interest, work, and even about yourself. So, the next time something unexpected blocks your way, find the wisdom hidden in the experience, learn, and it will guide you in the future. Have you observed that only when you see the lessons behind these minor hindrances will they stop appearing in your life? Of course, new problems will surface, but you will successfully overcome them with the same attitude.

Write off Limiting Beliefs

Limiting beliefs stay as opinions of ourselves that hinder us from chasing our goals, besides keeping us from doing important things to reach them. Simply stated, these are self-limiting perceptions that we have about ourselves and the manner the world functions.

An example is a belief that analytical people cannot be creative. This reminded me of a friend who is an accountant. After working diligently in her profession for almost three decades, she developed coronary heart disease. Advised by her doctor to balance work and life, she decided to have a career shift.

I remember having coffee with her eight years ago where I casually asked her future career plans. When she told me that she planned to work from home as a ghostwriter, I nearly choked on the coffee I drank. Before I can say anything, she smiled and said, *"I know what you are thinking. If you are good in numbers, you cannot be good in letters, right?"*

I nodded. It was then when my friend said, *"That limiting belief no longer serves me. So, I am writing it off in my career life."* Well, of course, I wished her well but feared what the future may have in store for her. After three years, while taking a walk at Times Square, I saw a vast digital advert of an online platform featuring its Top Ranked Freelancers.

Guess what? I saw my friend among those featured! I was so stunned that I dropped everything I was carrying. Suddenly needing some water to drink, I rushed to the nearest coffee shop. After taking a sip, I called to congratulate her. Up to this day, I cannot forget what she told me.

"Oh, it was not easy, but I knew it from the start. So, it didn't stop me at all. I kept learning, especially from my mistakes, and hone my skills. I may be among the Top Ranked freelancers, but the journey is still not near its endpoint. What is important is that I can now manage better my health condition while still earning a living."

You can easily see that my friend did not allow limiting beliefs to rule over her life in this little tale. She considered the scenarios that may have contributed to her health condition and thought of making amends. Perhaps, she imagined a career and lifestyle that can support her goals.

As for the intrusive thoughts that may have crossed her mind, she simply let them go. As a result, she could prepare and gather the energy needed to step out of her comfort zone. I am proud of having met someone who is a responsible author of her life story. So, why not do the same?

Claim your life by not holding on to limiting beliefs that you may have outgrown. When you see moments in your life as a chance to grow, you start rewriting your life story in a healthy and affirming way.

Acquire and Hone Skills and Qualities

By now, you are already aware of the skills and qualities needed to become a leader. So, which ones do you already possess? And what skills do you need to develop? For example, are you using your body language powerfully? Take note that communication is vital in leadership, and body language is a part of it.

If you need to work on your body language, perhaps using the "fake it until you get it" principle can help you. I have many friends who were able to boost their self-confidence by using it. You can have a quick start at maintaining eye contact when speaking to someone, smiling, and standing tall.

Simple as they are, they can noticeably make your self-image stronger and help you send the correct message to people around you. So, what must you avoid? Always stop yourself from frowning and having an icy facial expression. These can only send shivers down the spine of people. In short, be wary of your unconscious facial expressions. When in doubt, smile. That is enough to make the people around you know that you are approachable and self-confident.

Go for Powerful Goals While Focusing on the Broad Picture

More often than not, people follow leaders for the powerful goals they communicate. Thus, you must ensure that your goals are clear and that the people around you share your vision. Of course, this will require that you aim for the vast picture because it is very painless to get entertained by new vogues, markets, and projects.

In this way, you never leave behind the main picture as you proceed with your daily life. Remember that achieving and sustaining success takes self-control, focus, and staying clear on your priorities. When you spread yourself beyond the focal picture or start micromanaging, your work quality will definitely suffer.

Be in the Right Social Circle

This means that you are interacting with the right network. Still, this does not mean that you only surround yourself with like-minded people or those who think and behave just like you do. Actually, it is the opposite. The best approach to success is interacting with diverse people who are passionate and clever.

In this way, you get to listen to their points of view in detail. Well, yes, it can be awkward on your ego at times to agree that the most exemplary ideas do not come from you each time. Then again, you cannot deny that there are people who are actually more talented and experienced than you are.

Remember, influential leaders, not the copycat leaders, are more interested in getting desired results than looking good to other people. So go easy on yourself. Simply think that you are investing in education to stay sharp. After all, these, too, are important to leadership.

Seek a Mentor

If you are finding it hard to kick-start the process, you may consider finding yourself a mentor. When choosing one, make sure you can comfortably discuss your ideas or work, with him, besides asking for advice. This is important because passion has to be equalized by a sound judgment generated by years of involvement and repeated disappointments.

Of course, you can hang on until you gain the experience. Finding someone who will help you perceive things differently and possibly stop some costly blunders, however, is a wise choice.

The truth is, everybody holds the potential to become a leader, but to unleash it, you must first lead yourself. After all, you cannot naturally lead if you also need someone to show you the way. Turning your focus to yourself is never too late, regardless of age or stage in your career. Only when you get comfortable with yourself can you learn self-control, plan your path, as well as make sound choices.

When that happens, leadership will follow. When you have fully nurtured your self-confidence, and on your way to becoming the individual you like, it is time to shift your focus. It is already the perfect time for you to unleash the leader in other people. Never forget, learning the way to reveal to the world the finest in other people is among the most vital things you'll ever undertake as a leader.

Leadership skills may be acquired at any phase of your life. Knowing the skills and characteristics of good leaders and how a leader is different from a manager can build techniques for training yourself and colleagues, giving feedback, and surmounting specific organizational ordeals. We will now discuss a particular leadership style that I found very effective in the 21st century in the next chapter.

Chapter 7: Inspirational Leadership

The excellence of leadership in a group or business is frequently a deciding issue in its triumph. Though many workers respect and obey a senior boss because of his position within the company, the title alone is not an assurance that he will lead his people effectively. The most exemplary leaders always aim to motivate their people toward their respective professional and personal success while creating an ethos of motivation within their workplace.

Before we talk about the main topic of this chapter, let me first share with you some of the oldest and common leadership styles. I believe you are familiar with them as they are generally employed in various groups and businesses worldwide.

Leadership Styles

In management, there are many different leadership styles. Each style has its own place in a leader's kit of tools because a wise leader needs to know when to shift as the circumstances demand. Leadership styles exist on a band, such as the following:

Affiliative

Of all leadership styles, this leadership approach exists as requiring the leader to get at close range with people. It follows, therefore, that this leader pays attention and cares for the emotional requirements of his people. To do this, he strives to build a channel that links him to his team.

In the long run, this style stays all about inspiring harmony and founding collaborative relationships in teams. It is instrumental in smoothing clashes among members of the group or reassuring workers during stressful times.

Autocratic

This is perhaps the way most parents handle their children. Remember when your mom or dad simply tells you to do this as instructed? Generally, we follow because we look up to our parents as the most brilliant people in the whole wide world. So, as kids, they make the decisions without needing much input from us.

This command-and-control style lasts until we learn to share our views. Perhaps, this leadership style, considered old-fashioned today, did not last long because it does not value individual talents. Still, there may be certain situations when this leadership style is appropriate.

An example is when decisions must be instantly made, and only the leader knows the situation. Another example is when your team members are inexperienced or new. There is not much time for them to familiarize themselves with their work.

Authoritative

Though often confused with the autocratic leadership style, it is different. Here, your mom or dad would simply ask you to follow him or her. And, of course, you would do so as you see their confidence in mapping the way, besides setting expectations, while charming and energizing you each step of the way.

In moments of uncertainty, authoritative leaders boost clarity by helping them see the path they are taking, their goal, and what will happen once they reach it. Their main difference from autocratic leaders lies in their taking the initiative to give details of their thinking. Hence, they do not just issue commands but also allow their people to make choices and have the latitude to achieve the common goals.

Coaching

Coaches present different ways of approaching concerns because he views people by way of a pool of talent that needs discovering and developing. So, the leader unlocks this potential in people when he uses this leadership style. This, however, demands that the leader open his heart for people to be able to use his own power to tap the power within others. By giving people a bit of direction, the leader can help them draw out their ability to achieve all they are really capable of.

Democratic

If your boss asks your thoughts on some issues, then he is a democratic leader. This kind of leader shares info with workers about everything that can affect their work. Also, these leaders always seek the opinions of their people before making final decisions. As a result, this leadership style engenders trust and promotes team spirit and work from its members.

It welcomes creativity and facilitates the growth and development of workers. In the end, this leadership style makes it possible for people to do whatever the leader wants, but within a way preferred by the workers.

Laissez-Faire

The laissez-faire style remains the opposite of the autocratic style. It is the only one that involves the slightest degree of control. While the autocratic leader stands like a firm rock on concerns, the laissez-faire head lets people go with the flow. As a result, laissez-faire leaders appear to have so much faith in their people's ability but his lack of involvement can also make them seem aloof.

While it is beneficial to let people do as they prefer, a total absence of direction can make people unwittingly drift in the wrong direction. And when this happens, it goes far away from the critical goals of an organization or company. On the other hand, this style works well if you have a team of experienced and highly skilled employees who stand as self-starters and driven. To use this style effectively, leaders must monitor performance and give regular feedback.

Pacesetting

I view this by way of a spin-off of the autocratic style where the leader tells his people to do things as he does. This style is taken on mainly by a very bold leader who fixes the pace of work. Pacesetters put the bar of merit high and drive their people to run fast towards the goal.

While this style is helpful in terms of output and getting results, it can hurt people in the team. After all, we all know that even the best-driven employees can still become stressed in due time. Still, suppose you are an energetic business person working with like-minded people in a team on creating and marketing a new service or product.

In that case, this style can work well for you. Irrespective of your workplace, creative leaders exist beckoned to encourage success in other people. So, let me ask you. Of these leadership styles, which one best describes you? In any workplace, we require our heads to be fair, influential, and hardworking.

They must outshine others in their given roles while bringing out, as well, the finest in others, making sure their creative people have the support and resources to succeed. In reality, this is managing, but exceptional creative bosses do beyond simply managing people in their work.

They also challenge, guide, and inspire people to the point that they would voluntarily want to perform better and become better people. And this, I believe, is the essence of inspirational leadership.

Inspirational Leadership

This refers to the skill of positively influencing people and motivating them to become successful. Anyone at any level of experience can practice this kind of leadership, be they an entry-level employee or an executive. By practicing inspirational leadership, you can present your employees or partners the opportunity to foster their ambition founded on your attitude and actions.

Also called transformational leadership, this is a style wherein leaders encourage employees to transform and create a variation. This innovative change will then facilitate the growth and silhouette of the future triumph of an organization or company. As a result, inspirational leadership stimulates action, significantly lifts individual and group performance levels, besides igniting creativity and fearless innovation.

It truly lets loose latent skills by hitting into our innermost values and motivation and inspiring people towards following their passion, besides moving towards ambitious aims in life.

DOUBT

A Quick Walk in History

James MacGregor Burns was the first to propose this leadership concept. As a political author and leadership expert, he rendered inspirational leadership as evident when teams make each member proceed to an advanced level of driving force and morale. Through the gift of their traits and vision, these leaders inspire their people to adjust their prospects, views and drives towards working in meeting common goals.

Shortly, Bernard M. Bass, a scholar, enlarged the first ideas of Burns and made what is now known as the Transformational Leadership Theory. This altered concept is now defined founded on its effect on team members, such as the leader earning his members' trust, high regard, and respect.

Factors

1. Tailored Focus

Inspirational leadership involves giving positive support to each member. To foster helpful dealings well, these leaders maintain an open communication line for members to share ideas without any problem at all. In this way, the leaders can extend direct credit for the distinctive contributions of every follower.

2. Inspirational Stimulus

Transformational leaders possess a clear mental picture that they remain able to communicate to their followers. And this includes their capability to assist followers in experiencing a shared passion that drives them to fulfill goals.

3. Perfect Influence

The inspirational leader serves as a model for members to follow. And because the members respect and trust him, they pattern themselves after him and take on his ideals.

4. Mental Boost

These leaders challenge how things stand while cheering vision among members. This means that the leader inspires his members to hit upon new modes of carrying out tasks and novel prospects to gain knowledge.

Impact

Groups guided by an inspirational leader are prone to become loyal and likewise doing well. Perhaps, this is because the leader and members give much to the group and care straight up about the entire group's skill to meet goals. Needless to say, changes in team members are low to a certain extent because the leader can fire up lots of staunchness within his members.

As explained in the classic text, inspirational leaders inspire members to achieve great results that lead them to grow their own power to guide other people. These leaders help supporters grow and turn themselves into leaders through responding to the different needs of each that empowers them individually.

By aligning the objectives of each follower, the leader and the entire team share the vision of the larger group. Even researchers confirm the positive effect of inspirational leadership on a group, and thus, published it Psychology Today as an article. In the said article, Ronald E. Riggio, a leadership expert and psychologist, said that this happens because of the leaders' beliefs.

And these beliefs are that their supporters can perform well and lead others to feel inspired and energized. Leadership experts also suggest that a robust and affirmative concept of what is to come plays a vital role in becoming an inspirational leader. Still, the challenge exists, which is not only personally believing in this idea but also inspiring others to fall for your idea as well.

Hence, being genuine, sincere, supportive, and responsible are vital traits that will motivate followers to back your aims for the entire group. On top of that, one study also revealed the positive influence of an inspirational leader on the workers' well-being. Made known to the public through the Journal of Occupational and Environmental Medicine, this survey was completed on workers at different German companies on communication and information technology.

The scholars found out that workers who sensed a higher degree of inspirational leadership within their business owners or heads had conveyed higher health levels. So, what influence could such outcomes have for workers and bosses? The authors of various studies suggest that these results are vital. It helps firms create training programs to teach their people inspirational leadership skills.

Besides recognizing employees' needs and gaining communication skills, like resolving conflicts within the workplace, this kind of leadership can be of great help. Such coaching programs are seen as one more essential section of workplace well-being promotion and restraint efforts. Thus, this training should receive widespread support.

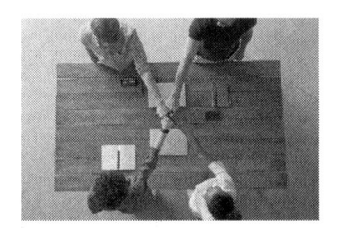

Benefits of Having an Inspirational Leader

If you are an inspirational leader, you can empower other people to have a zeal for their careers and find creative ways to accomplish their work. These leaders often devote time and effort to develop the gifts of those near them and help a firm flourish by showing their commitment towards their values and work. The multiple uses of this specific kind of leadership include the following:

Committed employees

Once employees catch a leader showing off a solid work moral belief, they frequently will aspire to give the same commitment level. Employees enjoy going to work with persons who enthuse them. As a result, they become loyal to a firm mainly due to their excellent and inspiring manager.

Increased engagement

These leaders foster a vibrant sense of drive to their group that helps every individual find added meaning in their function. By practicing this type of leadership, anyone can actually increase overall action among colleagues.

Meeting goals

Groups headed by an inspiring leader are more prone to meet, if not exceed, their target. And this is because inspirational leaders line up their function with team values, encouraging other members to set grand goals and get them done consistently.

Traits Common to Inspirational Leaders

Inspirational leaders drive their people toward going beyond their goals and motivating each member to their own best selves. They often do this by showing the skills, features, and mindset that they like their workers to demonstrate. Some of these traits possessed by inspirational leaders are the following:

Curiosity

An inspirational leader pursues learning and asks questions regularly. This interest can inspire other people to look for opportunities to grow as well.

Gratitude

People are extra prone to repeat fruitful behaviors often when they receive credits for their effort. By giving thanks and recognizing the way others offer you aid, you can move others to carry on utilizing their flairs.

Growth mindset

Inspiring leaders always inspire others to create chances for growth. They reveal a growth outlook and encourage people around them towards likewise doing so.

Integrity

This trait shows other people that they could depend on your good sense and have faith in you concerning sensitive issues. Putting integrity on view to see can build a trusting setting that inspires other people to uphold the same values.

Passion

To properly inspire other people, you must possess an ardor for the things you do, besides those you interact with. Genuinely looking after your company's goal and the welfare of your people helps to model this ardor that other people can seek as well.

Positivity

An inspirational leader maintains a positive mindset to properly increase office spirits. After all, positivity is a powerful driving force in a working team environment.

Tact

Being capable of handling a difficult circumstance with grace and tact can inspire other people as they bump into challenges. Thus, inspirational heads model insight to promote accessible communication and respect of others.

Developing Skills in Inspirational Leadership

Some leaders appear to possess a natural flair for inspiring other people. Still, there exist many ways towards developing your skills to become an inspirational boss. Here are the steps to facilitate your developing skills in inspirational leadership.

Know your people

People appreciate it once others devote time to be friendly with them, particularly in the place of work. By learning what your fellow workers value the most, as well as how they work at their best, you'll find unique modes to enthuse them. Different persons are moved by various stuff.

Knowing the individual traits of your group members will assist you in modifying your style of leadership when at work with others. When persons feel valued, they can become more easily inspired and guided.

Foster core values

To properly inspire a group, you require a reason representing the effort you do, besides guidelines for carrying out the work. Developing fundamental values and doing them each day will display to your group that their hard work can push positive changes in their existence.

Once determining your primary values, think of what is high of the essence to your group in their career and personal life. These core values can include innovation, creativity, community, hard work, and respect.

Build faith

By building faith in your workmates, you can create relationships that boost individual and group levels of growth. When a worker or colleague senses that he can rely on you, he may be likely to easily take your advice and help. An inspirational boss influences other people, and trust stays necessary for him to thrive. Confidence between coworkers displays that they support each other through challenges, besides succeeding with their team's best interests in mind.

Extend support

Inspirational heads readily offer aid to others even before being requested. Offering support helps in building a community feeling and encourages other people to accept more ambitious work. By making reserves readily available to other people, you can move them towards taking risks and keenly pursuing their career development.

Take charge

Taking responsibility on behalf of your shortcomings bares humility and capacity to learn that can inspire others. Mainly for people in an admin role, your keenness to accept faults and make changes for the better encourages others towards doing the same. Also, this strategy displays ardor and faithfulness to your group by prioritizing shared success over your own reputation.

Pay tribute to success

As inspirational leaders take responsibility on behalf of team setbacks, they also make out the team successes. Great leaders don't claim every merit on a job to get the high opinion of other people. Instead, they motivate their group more by giving out praise. Recognizing the moment an employee remains to do well and staying precise in your helpful feedback provides drive and the sensation of pride.

Next, we will discuss how you can proceed on your personal journey towards becoming an inspirational leader. We may also touch on some topics mentioned here, but this time, in more detail. So, let us continue…

Chapter 8: Your Personal Journey

The inspirational leadership style is highly effective once used appropriately; however, it may not be the finest choice for all situations. In some instances, groups may need a more autocratic style of leadership that involves keener control and more direction. And this is particularly required in cases where team members are unskilled, besides needing lots of oversight.

Then again, today's business settings are weighed down by challenges because of the changing human population and the worker prospects of a varied workforce. This can need a new type of leader who's a fusion of most leadership styles. As a Chinese proverb states, the wise adjust themselves to settings the same way the water flows. So, when you're thinking of improving your own skills in leadership, it would be best to evaluate your present leadership style.

Then, you can think of ways wherein your fortes can help the group you're leading. By assessing your own knacks, you'll be better at playing your strengths, as well as working on perking up your weak areas. To do this, you can follow this suggested process.

Know Yourself Using Reflective Thinking

Start by growing your knowledge of your main leadership style. This can be done in many ways. One way is asking trusted partners or members to define the strong points of your type of leading them. Another way is taking a leadership style review. Still, I highly suggest you learn reflective thinking.

It is a means of moving toward the function of becoming a leader through leading one's existence with presence, as well as personal mastery. Knowing to be mindful, aware, and attentive towards your experience with persons throughout each day exists as the focal point of this kind of thinking.

It draws near the study of leadership, besides practice, from the viewpoint of human knowledge. Based on the phenomena science, this leadership starts with reflection and self-awareness of one's involvement and other people and results in better communication that cheers and changes career practices.

Reflective thinking stays both an inner and outer process that helps self-understanding and better critical thinking flairs. It's more or less a type of internal work that brings about engaging within exterior work. It also remains a profound and necessary pursuit for seeing what is vital to oneself and in one's career or organization.

Thus, it is crucial to know one's thinking to properly understand oneself, besides making informed and cogent decisions when at work with others. Sequentially, paying attention to the ideas, feelings, and actions helps progress toward pulling off professional and business goals.

By thinking of one's life experience, we foster a fuller knowledge about what stands known and raises our potential as a leader. As an opening step to be a more insightful thinker, and in the end, a leader, I urge you to deeply consider the following questions:

1. What steps can you take to do reflective thinking?
2. What models, resources, and tools can help you to become additionally self-aware and thoughtful?
3. What do reflective thoughts in leadership stand for me?

A walk back in history will disclose that Wilson and Taggart developed the reflective thinking standard that points out the process of reflective thinking. Among the initial steps to it involves finding a problem, test, or dilemma. The next step calls for you to back off from the trouble and see the situation as an outsider to properly set up the problem.

This step involves watching, data gathering, thinking, and considering moral beliefs. These aspects assist in offering a mental image of your thoughts to outline the setting of the circumstances. The situation can be likened towards past events within a test to add up the problem, besides searching for possible answers within your range of understanding or experiences.

Then, it's time for you to ask yourself about what worked for you in similar circumstances you have met before and in what way is this circumstance different. Once you search for routine methods or identified likely approaches founded on reasoning over similar past encounters, predictions can be made, and some possible techniques are created.

The approaches exist then systematically checked with subsequent study and further checking. The final phase involves going through the actions chosen and the end results. Now, your question is if you feel that this situation is successfully resolved. When the approach is successful, a case in point is kept for future reference in similar instances.

If the method was unsuccessful, the problem would have to be framed again and the procedure repeated. Meanwhile, communication occurs inside the milieu of mindfulness. To effectively convey your thoughts, you have to be conscious of them. You can perhaps use the Awareness Wheel of Sherod, Miller, and Phyllis as a device for linking into yourself to become more self-aware.

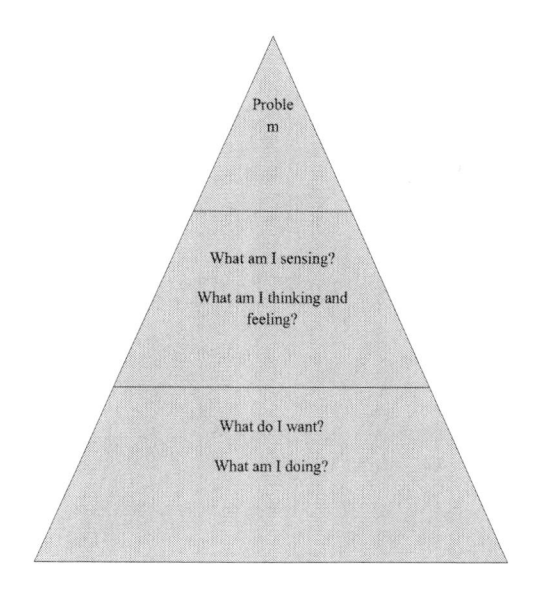

Another requisite to work effectively with other people is to be aware of your own distinctive gifts. This involves unique exploration. An assessment tool you can use is the Strengths Finder, which helps identify your talents, besides providing hundreds of approaches for turning them into fortes.

Reflective thoughts used in leadership take in a commitment towards the ongoing practice of frequent and sustained detailed self-awareness and growth while facilitating this complicated process in other people. As an insightful leader, you can share your deep thoughts with other people and ask them to also think things through.

It also involves listening to learn correctly from other people. This listening calls for an openness towards others that exists vital to social understanding and reaction. Listening fully, as well as reflectively, isn't obtained without hard work. It stays as an art and skill that have to be practiced, talked over, and refined.

If you wonder how leaders positively influence their work and develop their future leaders, this suggested process can help you. It can allow you to share your concerns with them while bringing out underlying and concealed issues towards the surface on behalf of yourself and other people involved.

It presents a chance for yourself and other persons to genuinely consider each other's points of view, forming some kind of release. This leads all involved to develop a broader view, a more excellent knowledge, and a renewed positive reception for one another. The reflective practice remains a transformative procedure.

Once the process of setting things right has transpired, all of you can move on in an extra unified manner. You can then set mutually agreed goals and a course of action that helps prevent future conflict. Activities like informal occasions to connect with each other and regular dates that encourage practice processes, besides opening communication channels, support leadership.

Choosing Your Leadership Styles

Finding out which leadership style is most fitting for you stands as a step to becoming a good boss. Developing a bespoke flair with the skill to spread out into other flairs as the case warrants may enhance your effectiveness as a leader. Before you can do this, though, you need to understand the various styles.

You need to be aware of the range of leadership flairs that can serve you well in each given situation. Then, find out what new knacks do you have to develop. When all set, you proceed by choosing to lead. Actually, you don't need to become a manager or team leader in cultivating skills in leadership. You can acquire these skills in your current job by:

Requesting for more tasks

While you would not want to request additional work in your first month on your job, it is better that you do not. Instead, do so once you have stayed in your position for some time and have become skilled at it. At that time, you can let your manager know that you are eager to develop your leadership skills.

You can then ask in what way you can assist. For example, you can ask your boss if upcoming projects are requiring a point individual. Or, ask if there is anything you can do on your manager's list of things to do.

Taking initiative

Look past the tasks listed in your work description. Continue thinking about what is good for your section and the business. Try to come up with ideas and compel yourself to work beyond the daily routine.

Targeting specific skills

If you possess a specific talent that you wish to develop, be it in communication or creative thinking, create a program to expand your abilities within this zone. This could denote taking lessons, finding a guru to help, setting a minor goal, or reading books that oblige you to build up this skill. Then, talk to your manager, co-workers, and friends not working in your office to assist in developing your program to improve.

Become Someone Others Opt to Follow

Valued leaders are aware that they cannot just stroll into a place filled with workers and say, "Hello! I am Boris, your leader. So, follow me." When you are the business owner, you can have this attitude, but the workers who follow you are forced to do so, and not because it is their own option.

They will listen to your advice, besides obeying your commands; however, it is unwished for followership based upon your organizational chain of command to a considerable degree. Leaders know that to really lead well, they have to attract those who wish to be keen on them.

So, how can leaders attract supporters? As a rule, leaders accept the need to draw followers. After all, having followers is important to understand leadership. To stay on, people have to feel convinced in the target to which the boss is going. For workers to possess this confidence level, the head must clearly communicate the comprehensive course, the key results desired, besides the principal schemes agreed upon towards reaching the outcomes.

The leader's next step is to enable and empower employees to perform their roles in meeting the stated goals. They hold the outline that they require to steer their individual actions. And inspired employees do wish to drive their personal actions. You'll fail in your leadership to your most exemplary employees when you forget this detail.

One more thing, it is a practice that makes a person a leader. To do this, you have to be honest with any method you use. For example, shifting from an authoritarian leadership style towards a different kind may be tricky at first. With practice, though, new behaviors eventually become natural.

Provide Inspiration and Future Vision

Understand that the current leadership vision is powerful due to the belief of the senior leaders in that vision and purpose. It is not just some words printed for hanging on the wall. This leadership vision can even be more powerful when people live in this vision every working day.

When leaders dole out a strong vision, organize, and put people in the workplace towards accomplishing it, a formidable dynamic drives worker performance. Once leaders walk the same way they talk, it is a demonstrated driving force for people. As soon as the leader shares a strong idea, employees will gather to it and may even choose the job within the company above other options.

As shown in the performance of employees, the leading idea is a retention reason for those sharing the vision. An example is when employees know that they are not just making wireless gadgets to make company owners rich but also providing a secure haven for battered women. To excite and inspire workers to willingly follow a leader, the idea set forth must:

1. Clearly fix organizational path and purpose;

2. Enthuse loyalty and consideration through the taking part of all workers;

3. Display and echo the unique fortes, culture, values, views, and goal of the group;

4. Inspire enthusiasm, trust, commitment, and delight in company workers;

5. Help employees become confident of being a piece of something larger than themselves or their work each day;

6. Be regularly shared and communicated, not just via reminders during company meetings and monthly announcements, but must permeate every communication at each organization level every day;

7. Work as the motive for why strategies are chosen, workers are hired, end users are selected, as well as products developed; and,

8. Challenge people towards outdoing themselves, stretching capacities, and reaching beyond set goals.

Thinking About the Present As If It Were the Past

An inspirational boss does not simply tell workers that he is deeply committed to their UX or customer's experience. Instead, he demonstrates this passion and commitment in every gathering, presentation, and within how he handles customer questions.

The leader's actions, therefore, inspire employees to behave similarly. Communication, integrity, presence, and sensitivity towards the requirements of the workers sum up the talents and features of an inspiring leader. Nobody is moved by any leader until they think he truly cares for them.

The skill to convey that passion, drive, and meaning towards others helps launch the inspirational ethos of your group. So, make others feel important, besides appreciated. If you believe that people are vital, you will act as a leader showing that belief. And when people feel important, they will work in stunning manners and think of how great a leader you are.

Live and Breathe in your Values to Ethically Behave While Developing an Agile Leadership Style

The best heads exhibit their core beliefs or ethics equally within their style of leadership and actions. When they are visible, this means that you are actually living them within your actions every single day. Lack of belief is a common problem in numerous workplaces these days.

And this happens when leaders never identify their ethics in the workplace. As a result, people do not know what to expect. In contrast, when leaders identify and share their values and live their values daily, it becomes visible to workers and will create reliance. Always remember that to say something and do something else can damage trust for a long time.

So, be an ethical leader by walking because of your talk and demonstrate why workers should trust you. According to Dr. Duane C. Tway, Jr., trust is a construct since it has three components. In his 1993 dissertation, "A Construct of Trust," he identified these components as (1) ability to trust, (2) perception of ability, and (3) perception of meaning.

Workplace ethics have the same path. Suppose the group's leadership holds ethical expectations and protocols. In that case, leaders can become a joke when they fail to meet the published code. On the other hand, leaders who exhibit ethical conduct powerfully impact the behavior of others.

Meanwhile, traditional leadership is still relevant within today's workplace. However, it may have to be fused with new styles in keeping with the way "leadership" is termed for this century. So, your leadership style founded on reflective thoughts should be blended with other types you may consider needed by the moment.

In this way, you can develop an agile leadership uniquely yours and serve your specific group's goals. In the process, you get to create a kinship wherein reflection exists as an acceptable way to learn and support each other. That is, once issues pop up, you can easily create a secure environment for thoughtfully sharing personal views. This will facilitate your tasks of setting goals, giving feedback, inspiring people, and endorsing self-monitoring.

Whatever blend of leadership styles you choose makes sure that you can draw your people's individual strengths. Also, give the workers various approaches to complete their work. On top of that, make it a habit to continually clarify or extend ideas while putting problems into the proper perspective. Seeking these things is essential towards helping to outline and tweak goals.

As a leader, it also helps to foster your preferred style of being. In this way, you can respond to leadership challenges daily by taking detailed and comprehensive mindfulness of (1) what type of leader you wish to be, (2) the kind of person you desire to be, as well as (3) legacy you want to give your people. In the form of a question, these can direct you to how you will take up the daily guidance of your people.

Among the most significant tests for leaders in our time is caused by rapid change. These trials require the leader to bring all his people to help shape the prospect through the cooperative exchange of ideas and joint action. So, be the inspirational and reflective leader who can model an agile capacity, manage clashes, and learn how to form and maintain relations.

Chapter 9: Setting Free your Team's Full Potential

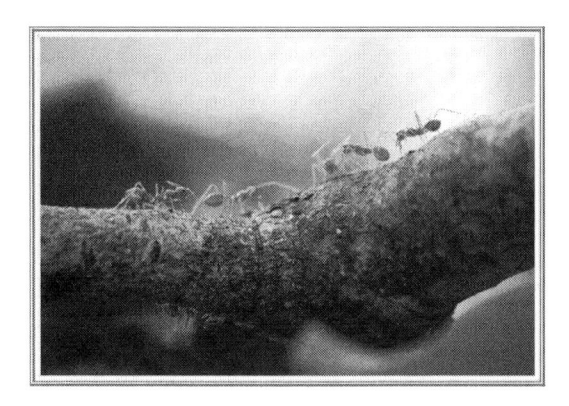

Unlike the ants shown in the image, humans are gifted with numerous means of becoming a leader. For many businesses, though, leadership development is quite costly in both time spent and monetary outlays. Still, most successful organizations recognize the importance of leadership and its impact on company profit and sustainability. For this reason, business owners and stakeholders encourage managers to have one-on-one talks around the potential of their staff and how team members can become inspirational leaders.

Before a leader can allow his people to spread their leadership wings with exciting work assignments, he must first work on his own leadership skills. Setting himself as a perfect example can clearly show his people possible career paths towards finding future opportunities they can work for. Remember, no blind man can lead another blind man.

So, if you wish to unleash the full potential of your people, then make sure to first improve your leading game. In any case, your people have only you to rely on for support and guidance. And, mind you, you cannot give something that you do not have or badly need yourself. Try imagining a leader who spends most of his time barking out commands.

Do you think this type of leader listens to his people? A person who does not listen can never ever discover what his team can offer. And if such is the case, how can anyone improve under his leadership? A true leader knows that success is judged based on the output and work of the entire team, not just on his own efforts. With that said, empowering staff exists as an essential chunk of a leader's job that assists them in bringing out their full potential. This is an inspirational leader's motivation amidst dealing with various types of persons having their unique behaviors, personalities, goals, and motivating factors.

Given such a challenge, inspirational leaders know that there's no one-fits-all process for leading a team. And this is where reflective thoughts come in to facilitate finding the right solution for each person led. This is very vital since encouraging the potential of each team member entails looking out for advancement chances at work when it arises.

Also, this helps push workers into the track of taking part in work that needs their knowledge and skills. Progress stays as a critical and essential part of all businesses, as it is for every staff. The inspirational leader must ensure that his team is offered practical and relevant training and growth options to properly work for improvement. Hence, all leaders need to run a working gap probe with their team to discover what training can meet the vital needs for the good of the person and the company.

And leadership does not end there. You have to keep honing and growing your own leadership style and abilities, as well. Let us now take a closer look at how you, as an inspirational leader, can unleash the finest in those you lead.

Communication

The initial place to begin is to boost your EI and soft skills. In doing so, you can communicate well with your people while developing empathy. In turn, this fosters trust since you are listening to whatever your people say and cannot say. The process will help you work on making an unstoppable working party using your leadership flairs.

By now, we all understand the weight of lucid communication when leading people. So, suppose you fail in this aspect. In that case, don't be surprised if you end up causing more that can range from an overall deficit in team competence and output to lack of trust. In worse scenarios, it can even lead to people feeling resentful of your ability to guide them.

Nobody can ever undervalue good communication skills to lead a team effectively, besides your team's ability to achieve their potential. Communication must always be clear, concise, and given candidly and genuinely. So, as an inspirational leader, you must promptly deliver critical information from the bosses to all members to avoid causing employee fears that some info is hidden from them.

Regular individual and group meetings

Conducting regular one-on-one and practical team discussions is a wholesome way to hold continuous and friendly communication. It also offers a familiar place and time for the members to share their thoughts and for you to remind them of how valuable their work remains to you, besides the business.

Since listening is another critical phase of communication, encouraging team dialogues where all can contribute is equally essential. In a one-on-one discussion, always ask for any concern that may be bothering your staff at work. In this way, you get to see the worker's priority in life and offer help before his problem can affect his work.

If the worker opts not to disclose anything personal, gently remind him that you understand and respect his reasons. Under any circumstance, the meetings should end with the workers knowing they can always run to you for guidance. And this can be anytime when they encounter unfamiliar situations at work or even in their personal lives.

This trust element is vital as this can propel them to progress with your guidance. And this includes taking the time to connect with your people. If you are not concerned with people on the human level, then you're off to starting wrong as a leader. A leader who's conceptually attentive to others but does not make time towards bonding with them misses the point, irrespective of these people being employees, colleagues, clients, or stakeholders.

Avoiding common leadership blunders

Being human, leaders also make mistakes daily. This often happens because they go through a lot of stress, lack specific knowledge, or develop bad habits. Knowing some common errors of leaders can help you be wary of them.

1. **Discouraging innovation and creativity**

Not promoting innovation and creativity shows that you, as a leader, are not focused on developing the assets and skills of your people. Too often, this happens when leaders focus entirely on pushing the success of company aims. And in the process of pushing, they deny the innate human craving to learn.

Have you met a person who does not want to grow his talents and expertise as he works? I haven't, and I guess you haven't, as well. Hence, understanding that learning exists as an integral segment of achieving outcomes is essential to all leaders. When you focus on education, you turn into a great boss who can see and develop flair in persons who might not even be aware of it. By encouraging innovation and creativity, you become, pretty simply, a leader who hunts for talent.

2. **Failing to give and receive comments, as well as setting clear goals**

People achieve above-average performance only when they are aware of their actual effectiveness. Sadly, leaders often turn their back on this need that robs persons of their leverage to the future. While harsh feedback is painful, great bosses know the proper way of delivering this pain within such a means that converts it into a benefit.

In reality, talented people who wish to learn prefers to be hurt with honest feedback than praised with falsehood. So, develop your skill to convey brutal truths about the work done and open the door towards higher performance.

3. **Micromanaging and failing to delegate tasks to the right people**

Doing this shows that you are managing activities, not leading people. Have you observed how many people cannot stand being treated like machine cogs? Yet, a lot in management is all about controlling, running, and planning actions, and as an extension, people.

In contrast, leadership involves inspiring and showing the finest in people by building trust and challenging them to take positive risks. The challenge here is for you to go beyond the role of a manager by focusing on people by way of them as people.

This requires delegating tasks to the right people and giving your people room to do the assigned job. I know this takes attention and time, but this can be done quickly with the proper bonding activities.

4. Missing the point of motivation

Most folks are guided by intrinsic reasons, such as being challenged, gaining new knowledge, making a key difference, or honing their talents. Unfortunately, too many bosses miss the chance to use this internal system. In its place, focus on external motivators, such as bonuses, promotions, cash, and artificial prizes.

Sure, you have to pay fairly for the services rendered, but always remember that such peripheral carrots can distort the intrinsic motivation system. You'll be a sounder leader once you aim at inspiring persons and tapping into whatever they genuinely want to attain about their respective growth and input.

5. Not considering emotions

Most substantial feelings are linked to loss, regret, failure, and parting. In fact, studies clearly show that loss, besides the dread of foreseen loss, drives people's behavior far more strongly as compared to potential rewards and benefits. So, leaders who pay no attention to the sentiments of disappointment and loss are really making a significant slip-up that powerfully brings down employee engagement. By simply knowing these emotions and showing genuine concern for your people's experiences, you can create a vast difference.

6. Opposing change

Lacking change, our groups, like everything else in this world, wither and die in the end. Leaders who do not drive change position their businesses in danger. If you do not explain the advantages that the change can bring will naturally make people resist change.

In general, people resist the unknown out of fear or possible pain it might cause with the shift. As an inspirational leader, your job exists to become a safe haven that offers a feeling of safety and encouragement to explore. Stated differently, you must feel enough concern to nurture courage from your people.

Strengthen communication channels and work culture

First, seek to consolidate your external and internal communication channels as one. Speeding up these exchanges helps reinforce the idea of belonging to one team where all work together toward similar goals. In the process, you are encouraging helpful work culture.

In reality, you are fostering an ethos where vocalizing ideas and flexibility are not just the standards. They are encouraged and provide chances for your people to display their unique talents or strengths. The perfect example of this is when leaders initiate fun activities, such as hosting a singing or dancing contest.

This is among the many ways you create room for your people to seek the best in themselves. So, never get tired of giving your people the right experiences. As you give out work assignments, consider the unique tasks you hold requiring flairs that your people may not know, but should, when they want to go up the corporate ladder.

Then, find a way for your people to start having exposure in those spaces. For example, you give a monthly presentation to newly hired personnel to explain what your department does in the company. It is a relatively easy task but not typically done by your people.

To facilitate them gaining that experience of talking to a crowd, you may consider asking them to observe your presentation. Eventually, you can request one staff after another to present in your place. Similarly, you can apply this to other tasks that your people may need experience in, such as running meetings or overseeing projects.

Since these duties typically include dealing with other people, you will need to ensure that the team remains on task, reach objectives, and collaboratively works. And, yes, all these skills are essential to a leader.

Coaching

Coaching is a valuable means to help people achieve more excellence in sports, life, and career. In the office, coaching supports carrying out tasks and helps bring out the potential in every employee. It allows individuals to perk up their communication knacks, adjust to shifts, and develop different productive behaviors.

Also, coaching inspires constant learning to improve output. In fact, a study revealed that managers or leaders who went through training in line with coaching after training saw an 88% productivity increase. When delivered within the right setting, coaching can offer your employees the focus, response, and support of newly-learned actions necessary to get ahead and thrive. Effective coaching entails the following components:

Connect

Fixing the proper framework and environment aimed at coaching employees exists as the first thing to do. Coaches have to hook up with individuals to properly help them. By showing commitment towards their employees' individual growth, coaches help them unite with the coaching benefits, further motivated to see through objectives.

Coaches link with people by questioning them to get them to think and talk about their encounters, providing hints that the mentor can use by way of developing the coaching process. It stays at this vital step that the mentor sets the manner, establishes trust, and sets the coaching context with employees.

Once again, scheduling frequent one-on-one meetings is a priority in this stage, despite how packed the leader's schedules are. Unquestionably, it's the best method for learning more concerning your employees, especially on what inspires them and what hidden talents they may possess.

Also, it allows you to provide constructive feedback and exchange ideas within a less official setting. Most importantly, individual meetings let you assign the correct goals, incentives, and tasks to precise people. In this manner, you can motivate them well and hand over specific responsibilities towards the right people.

What is more, it offers the chance for you to connect certain people with the appropriate people. Leaders who unleash the full potential in others remained called multipliers because they pull persons into their circle with the frank understanding that hastened development is a portion of the task.

And since they also search for talent all over the place and make out that deep brains are shown in many diverse ways within a company, they devote time to know each person's skills. In this way, they can easily connect them with the proper persons and the right prospects to build a virtuous series of value, growth, and openings.

Thus, leaders create networks that transcend work. This can be observed when they encourage clients towards participating in traditionally in-house events, meetups, conferences, drinks after work, summer parties, besides Christmas get-togethers with the workers.

This only shows how necessary bonding is. After all, it stands as a deep open connection that exists different from merely liking someone. What's more, you don't have to adore someone to connect with that person. All that's needed exists for you to become acquainted with him and know what works best for him.

And, of course, that takes some time beyond pure work. At the end of the day, people want that feeling of belonging, making bonding a critical fragment of forming rapport. Emotionally connecting, as well as creating synergy, breeds even more drive. In fact, research reveals that most persons tend to be irrational as they base most of their choices and judgments on emotions. People also dread loss, which I've already pointed out as a more powerful reason than potential gains. Thus, playing to avoid loss can motivate people.

Observe

A good coach observes, besides asking key delving questions before identifying concerns and advising. An example is when an executive coach communicates three mindful questions asked after seeing a staff complete a task, do a presentation, or direct a meeting.

These questions are (1) what went all right? (2) What failed to meet expectations? (3) What will you do in another way if you are given a chance to do it all over again? These questions can help the person coached to see chances for improvement. In contrast, the coach begins to make a roadmap aimed at improving his performance.

This stage can help a coach define what a suitable member is to his team; thus, making them play an extremely influential part in team development. Yes, there are no shortcuts, yet you can facilitate the unleashing of their full abilities and adjust them toward adeptness by observing them well.

When observing them, make sure of the correctness of their perception in terms of the communicated purpose and objectives. Ensure each of them understands their role, assigned tasks, and how they can contribute to overall success. This phase is also crucial in your regular review of team development.

> We rise by Lifting Others

Highly fecund groups and their members hold an edge against their colleagues. They are the business asset because they firmly produce clearly defined results to the firm that make them feel happy at work. As a result, they find it often stress-free to split their duties, making them less frazzled in the office.

For this reason, the leader must watch workers aimed at finding out what inspires teams and members to become highly productive. Since various things enthuse each person, leaders should seek to boost and provide the correct kind of inspiration. And all this requires the leader to be very observant.

Assess

Coaches help their people unleash their potential by measuring their behavior. To do this, coaches depend on assessments towards measuring the style of making decisions, openness to advice, and the individual's approach towards ambiguity. An evaluation, such as 360-degree feedback, may help a coach know how someone exists perceived by people around them and describe how the person's performance equates to the challenges and demands of his job.

When the review feedback is gone over with the person, the coach helps him know the changes required to address the input taken from his direct superior and peers. Useful tools aiding coaches during this stage include 360- or 180-degree feedback tools, multi-rater behavior reviews, surveys, feedback forms, assessment of traits on the internet, and other channels. By assessing work, you can find the areas where the staff needs to improve and even suggest the moving up the best workers.

It can also be the basis for you to commend the effort and give rewards for those who always do well and even exceed expected outputs. Team and member outputs are observed, measured, as well as assessed by using work managing systems. Of course, top performers are recognized, while those consistently doing well are rewarded for inspiring them further.

Without such recognition and incentives provided, workers may feel discouraged to level up their performance. Also, rewarding top workers can have a domino effect in motivating other workers and teams to enhance their performance to properly earn that credit.

Regularly satisfying good work can definitely raise the excellence of work all over the organization. When people are aware that they may get a promotion, they will perform better. This is something that business owners should definitely consider when they want their business to grow, right?

Other ways of rewarding employees for exceeding work expectations could also take the form of free food, vacations with pay, presents, or rare options like VIP tickets to sport or concert events. The key here is to balance the gift or reward with the worker. For example, giving a top performer an NFL ticket may sound excellent.

Still, if the said person has zero interest in sports, the reward may be worthless, right? So, to encourage someone to continue unleashing his full potential, you must know what is important to him.

Clarify and talk things out

Clear feedback stays as the only means for workers to understand the what, process, and why of change. Coaches can offer clarity on the objectives and results of earning is through a training meeting debrief. When members probe with an expert facilitator after every training activity, they translate into real-world outcomes.

As a result, the members can realize how their behavior could be adjusted, if not improved, to level up their performance. Another method to practice explaining remains through an activity, like coach-the-builder. In this exercise, an individual is a builder of a block or Lego structure.

He goes through the building process following the direction of a delegator who's relaying info from the designated leader. The leader views what the building looks like only upon the completion of the activity. In this activity, people learn the value of listening wisely, asking helpful questions, and delivering useful information while working jointly to reach the shared goal. Of course, providing and gathering feedback is essential at this stage.

Feedback is vital in improving talent and skills, especially when timely, helpful, and constructive. It has to be offered thoughtfully and aimed at performance improvement, not to criticize workers.

Change

Coaching explains, imparts, and shows how to lessen the gap amid actual and required work output. When a person makes out the chances for stepping up, the coach arranges for guidance that urges change in actions. Also, coaches can display the means to model new conduct and use them often at work.

An example is when a person receives mentoring to improve interaction with his team that he can immediately apply while working. When given in the correct setting, coaching is an effective means to help workers unleash their top abilities. With experiential coaching, employees learn the manner to model innovative behaviors by execution.

After training, you can use this model to shore up experiential learning by providing critical advice and support towards helping employees while practicing freshly learned behaviors. Once experiential training is secured by a mentor who connects, watches, assesses, and clarifies, besides providing how-to instruction, the potential of the workers is unleashed, and performance rockets. People don't naturally resist transformation but resist the dread of uncertainty and possible pain. In the process, it would appear like they do not welcome change, although the issue is not really that. If you devote time to assist them in realizing the demand to change and its potential gains, most people will accept it.

It will also teach them to see every change as an avenue to create something positive. And when we focus our thoughts on optimism, it helps us cash in on the change. Wondering why? The answer is quite simple. Note that forming bonds indeed entails a loss in the future as most relationships do not stay long enough.

Thus, bonding chases a cycle. It begins with people forming attachments because of the comfort it brings. It may start with a mutual interest causing the bond that may eventually weaken and lead to a grieved loss. For this reason, several people don't connect in any possible way with other people to sidestep the future pain caused by the loss.

Still, grieving losses let us move on, forming new attachments or bonds, which relaunches the cycle. Let's face it. Today's organizations cause plenty of hurts due to changes in jobs, redundancies, restructuring, advancements, change in office space locations, or even depressing feedback. Unrealized prospects can also form a sensation of loss. Hence, although leaders promote connections, they also value the impact of loss and give room for workers to grieve.

Training

Training provides you the tools needed to help yourself and your people to touch up performance and succeed. As you have now identified the areas where you and your people need to improve, you may choose the type of training that suits the needs. Still, finding the correct balance between various ways of gaining knowledge that suits everyone is a challenge.

For example, the 70:20:10 standard suggests that 70% of learning occurs through experience, like daily tasks; 20% is through talking with others, such as when you speak with your coach; and 10% is through fixed training courses. In training, you have to give your people the chance to utilize the knacks they have to develop, talk about them with highly experienced practitioners, besides training them appropriately.

Purpose

For career advancement, learning stays critical. And for this very reason, people like to join organizations that possess high knowledge and development capabilities. Meanwhile, an active training and development structure can help spot and fill gaps in skills within the group.

> YOU DIDNT COME THIS FAR TO ONLY COME THIS FAR

It can facilitate individuals to acquire competencies that can improve work excellence. Also, it can make them ready for leadership or for them to accept new future responsibilities. Additionally, it aligns the career growth objectives of the workers with the business purpose.

Given the reasons why training is essential, needless to say, developing existing fortes and maintaining an open setting is imperative in growing your team. Bear in mind that this involves encouraging your people to take a step off their area of comfort. It's a fact that people usually put down their roots in the mundaneness of their daily work.

Of course, it is easier for them not to bother exploring other things. As a result, some workers need some pushing to try doing a new duty or learn some new stuff. So, to see whatever else people can do and perhaps excel in, the leader must encourage them to step off their area of comfort every now and then.

In this way, they can discover any concealed talents or flairs that they might not know they possess. Since this is an excellent chance for people to draw out their fantastic potential, leaders must lead and train well. Come to think of it, many people say that when they leave a company, it is because they want to be free of their bosses.

I remember talking with a friend who said the very same thing. After three years of working with a prestigious company, she left because she found it very difficult to bow to leadership not invested in her career development. She also found it difficult to trust a leader who lacks professional, leadership, and occupational skills!

In our friendly tete-a-tete, I was amazed to hear that she had to take on some of that leader's duties just to make sure her department runs well. No business owner can demand more good output from his employed people when they are not provided with a leader they can rely on for support and guidance.

Therefore, it's vital for bosses to keep honing their skills and knowledge and not become complacent. Also, they must work with their people to assist them in establishing and achieving their professional development goals. This entails using authority helpfully, teaching people to turn letdowns into opportunities to learn, and helping them to stretch their limits. Since training cost is high, it would be best to start using a predictive review tool.

Process

Many firms end in tears in the appraisal of foretelling leadership talent. Focused tools get rid of the penchant of decision-makers to pick upcoming leaders who very much resemble themselves and weed out people who poorly fit leadership roles. So, before deciding on an assessment tool, leaders or major stakeholders must agree on what success appears to be for every leadership role, besides aligning those flairs and traits to success work factors.

The leadership knacks and disciplines you will assess should be focused on the future to safeguard that your high makings can fulfill a strategy as you move forward. Most reviews will also look at a person's previous and present actions at work. This is important in knowing why people act in a specific manner, when, and where they are most prone to behave in the same way in the future context.

Standing up for a learning essence within the group sends a strong message that raising your leaders exists among your most serious concerns. And when you coach them, make sure to train them to become coaches. After all, coaching is a leadership skill. One form of teaching common to many companies is having an annual team-building event.

Exercises during this event are fun and practical ways to boost teamwork and spot people's weak points and strengths. Just make sure to select the activities very carefully to ensure meeting your training goal. To do this, identify first your team's main challenges. For example, when you notice poor communication is causing your team to make mistakes or miss deadlines, pick activities that improve basic communication skills.

These activities must cover the skills that promote empathic listening, understanding nonverbal cues, and public speaking skills. Specific team-building exercises encourage creativity, develop leadership, strengthen problem-solving skills, and build team planning skills.

So, choose your activities well and pick those that you are comfortable participating in. Your people may want to see in you the potentials of the exercise, besides modeling the actions you wish to develop in them. Training may also be done through implementing job rotation.

Provide those with high makings direct practice by switching them through various roles and work within the group. The point here is to dare, push, and expand the level of their skills. Place them in new posts, furnish them with new duties to expose them to unique deftness, and add to their know-how. Also, organizations must consider different data types when planning a leadership growth scorecard to assess the success of leadership growth programs and events, such as the following:

1. Application of skills of a leader in various job positions;
2. Business effect of applying knowledge and innovative skills of leaders;
3. Intangible benefits linked to business dealings, like work climate, work attitudes, and resourcefulness, which do not have monetary values.
4. Learning and acquisition of skills and knowledge on leadership;
5. Participants' satisfaction level with leadership growth activities and plans;
6. Return on investment or ROI measuring up monetary gains with program expenses; and,
7. Signs of the range and capacity of leadership growth.

Of course, many of the comments on the success of the leadership growth plan will be subjective. After all, a leader can see that what worked well in his case may not work for others even when followed to the letter. Still, the supreme leadership growth goal is to boost the volume of people to become good in the roles and pursuits of a leader.

Focal Points

A leadership growth plan to become truly useful must align with the group's business approach and offer chances for growth fitted to its every worker. These growth plans may focus on:

1. **Emotional intelligence**

EI describes a person's skill to be caring and thoughtful of other people's feelings, besides dealing with his own feelings and whims. In the long run, leadership growth exists almost to boost a person's EQ or emotional intelligence percentage. Tackling this job in a team setting is mainly good because lots of EI becomes known within the social context. In fact, 99% of top workers have been found in studies to possess high EI levels.

2. **Group-based leadership**

This helps workers get real-world skills online. In reality, this leadership growth process can occur over varied methods, such as outside contact with a public group, trade or career factions, and in-house or outside training programs. This requires leaders and future leaders to acquire or hone skill sets in making decisions and offer each other valuable and helpful feedback. The list also includes boosting social interaction, breaking working silos, and tackling real-world trials online.

3. **Leader-to-leader**

Pairing senior leaders with new ones or practicing coaching in the group can cause gains like knowledge transfer, confidence support, and open teamwork, among many others. In this way, skilled leaders help others know the inner works of the leading team and offer a unique viewpoint to future leaders within a group.

4. **Stretch duties, work experiences, and shifting tasks**

Among the best modes to vet for leadership, besides growing leadership skills, stays through stretch duties. These may bring about reassignment towards a different geographic location, business division, or functional unit. In this manner, people are tempted to take a step away from their comfort areas and challenged towards employing new approaches to manage change.

Future trends

An education company, specifically the Center for Creative Leadership, has identified trends for upcoming leadership development plans, as follows:

1. **Collective leadership**

More fluidity and less hierarchy in workplaces will demand a wider distribution of leadership skills across the staff.

2. **Individual ownership**

Well-known models depend on organizational arrangements, including workforce, to sponsor and coordinate leadership growth initiatives. Still, the most robust gains are realized once the workers can determine their personal training plan.

3. Innovation

More excellent quickness and testing are needed towards meeting the challenges of different environments.

4. Vertical development

This development contrasts to the traditional focal point, called horizontal development, which reinforces the fundamental competencies needed to perform well at the current level. Although that's still important in the future, the vagueness of the evolving work world will demand more substantial stress on building the leadership capacity of workers in more complex roles.

Finally, let me remind you that leaders manage rapid changes caused by new tools, global markets, affairs of states or nations, ecological concerns, and conflict. As such, they must transform their people's deep beliefs and mindsets to create group volume aimed at helpful change. Thus, it follows that leadership growth is a crucial human resource challenge today that will remain even in the next decade.

Leadership growth encompasses prescribed and informal teaching. So, becoming an experienced leader is like turning into a skilled professional where application and training are critical. At the end of the day, we become inspirational leaders only by using our learning, knowledge, and involvement in our daily lives. And this calls for group decision-makers to set down a good path for people to learn, develop, and succeed.

Conclusion

Indeed, a leader can give people what they may wish within their skills. As expected, he may not provide a salary raise when the business isn't reaching its profit goals. In contrast, though, he can share rewards when the firm is earning well. And to make this possible, the leader must inspire his people to do their share in the work needed. Also, the leader knows that, although money urges people to work hard, praising, giving gifts, and saying thanks, work in the same way.

In fact, making out the worker's input to a worthwhile project and speaking frankly to him about his work's value to the firm is already a starting place for inspiration for him. Thus, actions taken every working day by leaders aiming to inspire others are with purpose. We cannot deny that the tremendous speed of change in these times creates significant tests for the growth of new leaders.

These trials press counter to the human skill limits both for leader runners and those charged with inspiring new leaders. Although the demand to develop innovative, thoughtful, and inspiring leaders are known and actively followed, significant personal and institutional obstacles may hinder accomplishing this target. Generally, institutional obstacles include limited time and funding and secondary top management backing when it comes to mindset and priority.

Many firms also lack the stanchness in fostering the right organizational culture. It is sad to note that leadership development events are too lacking in strategy and planning. Perhaps, this is because many companies today lack administrative and coaching systems. On the other hand, some obstacles faced by people in leadership development include personal ability to hold on to and use leadership knowledge and skills in changing circumstances, lack of following through development activities, and generational differences within values, communication, as well as an understanding of tools, to name a few.

Despite these hindrances, I strongly advocate a more tremendous effort to develop inspirational leaders. What's more, today's dynamic working environments put a dire need to making sure a strong leadership pipeline remains handy for the years to come. As we continue living in uncertain times, isn't identifying, selecting, and training the best likely leaders a critical strategic goal for safeguarding a sustainable, driven organization?

With that question to ponder on, allow me to end this book, which I hope can enrich your knowledge in the value of inspirational leadership in today's world. Thank you for getting a copy of this book, and may it constantly remind you of why you choose to read it in the first place. Perhaps, you may not be aware of it before. Still, by reading this book, you are actually launching into the journey of becoming an inspirational leader. And if there's something I can confidently say to you right now, that is, the world needs more leaders like you…

-- Zack McQueen

Made in the USA
Coppell, TX
06 September 2022

82692774R00059